Dedicated in love
to
Joanna and Zachary

To My Readers

I offer this work to you as a gardener works with the earth. For some, reading this message may be painful, as your soil is being tilled and cultivated.

For others, life experiences have already prepared you for new growth, as mine had. For you, this book may sow new seeds.

For still others, your seeds have been sown and may need only these waters of encouragement to grow stronger.

And, finally, to those of you who are blossoming, living each day in joy and gratitude, may this book be a celebration of your life's beauty and a reaffirmation of how far we have come.

No matter what shape your personal secret garden is in, my prayer is that this work will bless and stretch you, generating a desire to share the seeds of hope with others.

Acknowledgments

Thanks to my loving and patient children, Joanna and Zachary. Your hugs kept me going!

Special thanks to Mom and Dad, who taught me how to risk, and who have courageously grown and shared so much from their own journeys. I love you both very much!

Thanks to my wonderfully supportive friends: Sarah Ruma and my Earth Angels Women's Group: Marti, Mary Lynn, Becky, Sandy. Also to Teresa Cunningham, Carol Dyvig, Jim Scholz, Stephanie Lorenz, Mary Beth and Tom Burton, Mike Bloomingdale, Cathy Beck, Karl Hillie, and Barb Vasiloff. I'm so blessed to have had each of you in my life!

To my see-ers: Madelene Rose, Krissa Lee-Regier, Chris Murphy, and my editors and readers: Ada Hale, Kay Palmcook, Kate Brennan, Tom Schulte, Wes Sime, Tom Bockes, Jim Rippey, Dawn Arnold, Elaine Wells, Peg Callaher, Katie Pogge, Rebecca Rotert, Beth Wells, Maryann Miller and Kathy Havlik. Thanks for your wonderful insights and assistance!

Also, this book is filled with stories of the thousands of seminar participants who courageously transformed their lives and shared their journeys with me. To all of you, I am most grateful.

Finally, I live each day in gratitude to the God of all creation who knows me completely, loves me unconditionally, and works all things for good. Honor and Praise be Yours!

Taking Care of Me: The Habits of Happiness

by Mary Kay Mueller

I. Introduction

II. Getting A "Head" Start

III. The Four Reasons We Run From Happiness

IV: The Twelve Habits Of Happiness

V: Shift Happens - Tools For Transition

INTRODUCTION

Things do not change: We change.
Henry David Thoreau

The First Day Of The Best Of My Life

On August 8, 1986, I fled to a domestic violence shelter with my two-year-old daughter.

As soon as we arrived, I began to question my right to be there. Most of the other women had broken jaws or cracked ribs. My six-foot-two husband had only knocked me down to prevent me from leaving the house. Still, I had told him, "If you do that again, I'll leave you." When it happened again the next day, I realized I had no choice and left.

"Welcome, Mary Kay," the counselor said, as she offered me a chair in her small office. Her steady gaze and silver hair were reassuring. "I want to go over some rules with you. One of our counselors will show your daughter to the room where you'll be staying."

A million questions raced through my mind, as I nodded and released my two-year-old's hand.

"First, do not tell anyone the location of this shelter," the woman continued. "This is a safe haven. You could endanger women's lives."

Again I nodded, trying to let it all sink in.

"The second rule is just as important. For these next four weeks, you may not talk about your husband. You may not so much as mention his name. Do you understand?"

Dumbfounded, I stared at her. "Then what are we going to talk about?"

The naiveté of my question exposed how little I understood about self-esteem and empowerment, subjects I had taught in my high school speech classrooms for years. Yet none of the texts had covered the basic truths of life I was about to learn, at age 34, in a women's shelter.

During the next four weeks, my way of looking at myself and at life altered radically. I realized that living to make others happy was fruitless, for no one can make anyone else happy. Therefore, I set out to learn how to be happy myself.

When it came time to leave, the most difficult person to say good-bye to was the silver-haired counselor I had met the first day, whom I had now come to love and trust completely.

"How will I ever thank you for all you've done for me?" I asked through my tears.

"You will share the message," she answered.

And so I have. First, with five neighborhood women at a weekly support group I called ***Taking Care of Me.*** Listening to their stories, I knew I was not alone. These women told of giving away their personal power to their bosses, spouses, parents and children. All of us needed to get back in touch with ourselves.

Using what I learned in the shelter and from leading the group, I developed a program that improved every aspect of my life: my mental and physical health, income, relationships, and spirituality. To date, I have shared what I've learned with over 20,000 men and women in corporations, hospitals, schools, and churches throughout the country. It is my great joy now to be sharing it with you.

The Courage To Begin

Congratulations on beginning! Investing in yourself by reading this book is a very important and healthy step.

Ask yourself:

1) What kind of person tends to go to a gym regularly? A healthier person or a more sickly one?
2) What kind of person goes to church or synagogue regularly? One with stronger faith or weaker faith?

We all have a "hope-muscle" that needs to be exercised and strengthened from regular workouts. Keeping our hope and faith muscles in shape makes good sense. Reading this book and doing the exercises will provide you with a format to help discipline yourself in these areas.

In the meantime, know that those who study self-esteem and empowerment often have higher esteem than those who do not. A lower self-esteem individual feels powerless over his or her life. You, on the other hand, believe you can make changes in your level of happiness and health. You are absolutely right!

Throughout this text, I will be offering optional exercises for you to write out or share with a friend. My experience with teaching this material indicates that you'll benefit 10 times more from this material if you stop and complete these exercises. The greater the risk, the greater the reward!

Who Is This Book For?

This material is useful for teenagers to adults. It will be extremely beneficial to those who:

- Have a challenging time standing up for themselves, setting limits, or finding time for what they want to do.
- Take better care of others than they do themselves.
- Aren't sure what they want in life or what their gifts are.
- Have lost track of their priorities in the busy-ness of life.
- Are in a time of transition in roles, relationships, or responsibilities.
- Want to get out of blaming and take charge of their lives.

This book is *not* recommended for those in the early stages of grieving, which can include any time from 1 to 12 months after a death or divorce. The need at this time is more to let grief out than to take information in. However, each individual is unique, so listen to your own needs.

Finally, for those on medication or seeing a counselor, this book is not meant to be used as a substitute for either. Rather, it works well as a supplement to counseling or support groups. If you have considered suicide in the past year, I do not recommend this material without the support of regular counseling appointments.

Using This Book In A Group

I find I make longer-lasting lifestyle changes if I have made a commitment to do so with other people. If you are like me in this regard, this text can be a workbook for an ongoing small (five to eight persons) group experience, such as the one I created in my neighborhood. I suggest you begin by meeting on a certain day each week or every other week for a few months and then reassess your group's needs.

I also suggest some rules for your get-togethers, such as:

- We will own responsibility rather than blaming others for our circumstances.
- We will give advice only when it is requested.
- We will refrain from labels or put-downs of ourselves and others, as in saying someone is "stupid."
- Humor is fine as long as jokes are not teasing put-downs or used to distract the group from the topic.
- We will only discuss concerns of the people in the room.
- We will keep all shared information confidential.

One of the advantages of sharing in a small group is the awareness that you are not alone. This feeling of "normalcy" has a relaxing effect that will aid in achieving greater self-acceptance. The other advantage is simply this: If you hear the same concepts echoed by other members of a healthy share-group, you will learn them faster.

My final suggestion about forming a small group is not to let meetings become broken-record sessions where you return each week or month to share the same stories. Expect growth and movement from each participant. The 12-step movement (AA, NA, OA, etc.) encourages a practice of becoming a sponsor for others once you have been in the group awhile. This is an excellent way to keep yourself working a program in a fresh, new way throughout your recovery.

Support groups are simply a boat
to get us to the other side of the lake.
When we get there,
we start using our stories for attention, pity, or power.
At this point, it's time to get out of the boat.
Carolyn Myss, author of *The Creation of Health*

Using the program described in this book, groups have been meeting for up to four years on a regular basis. None of them has had a facilitator. They honor the wisdom of each person equally, although some members hold prestigious positions and others have multiple degrees. While facilitated groups serve an important need in every community, this is a book about self-empowerment. Shared leadership is one of the best ways to discover hidden gifts.

No matter how you plan to use this material, know that your **intention** to succeed is the most important component. Therefore, do not judge yourself during this process, but consider doing as I did, keeping a record of your triumphs and setbacks. It will be a powerful record of your life journey.

God Bless!

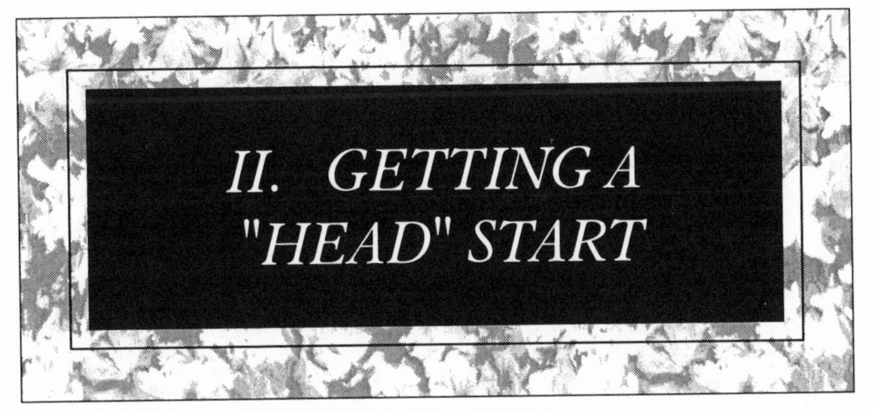

People are just about as happy
as they make up their minds to be.
Abraham Lincoln

The Phrase That Changed My Life

I could hardly believe what I was hearing from the counselor that first morning in the shelter.

"While you are here, we will talk only about you. He is not the problem. You are. We believe there are no adult victims, only volunteers."

"You're saying I chose this?" I asked.

"In a way, yes."

"Why would anyone run from happiness and choose misery and chaos?" I demanded.

"That's a very good question, Mary Kay. You'll be here for four weeks. You'll have plenty of time to think about it. I'm sure you'll find the answers you're looking for."

And so I did.

"No adult victims, only volunteers," initially sounded like the worst possible news. It was actually the best possible news. If I was the problem, I was obviously the solution. Once I accepted the premise that I had the power to choose, I realized I could continue to volunteer to live in fear, misery and chaos; or I could volunteer for happiness, health, and more loving relationships.

The Fundamental Belief

In a 10-year study by the National Institute on Aging, it was found that the happiest people in the world had a variety of attributes in common. The most important happiness factor was "**...the belief that they had the power to take control of their lives.**" This concept of personal responsibility and power became the foundation for my recovery program.

The process of owning our power begins with the realization that we have within us the cure for what ails us. This awareness forces us beyond blaming circumstances or other people for our predicaments.

People are always blaming their circumstances.
I don't believe in circumstances.
People who get on in this world
are the people who get up and look for the
circumstances they want,
and if they can't find them, make them.
George Bernard Shaw

Many people believe that buying into this paradigm of "No Adult Victims" would bring more pain than they could bear. So they live with half-truths and half-heartedly move through lives half-full of useless suffering and chaos.

When Life Turns Up The Heat

The results of a laboratory experiment done in the '60s illustrates this point. When frogs were placed in a pot of hot water, they jumped out instinctively. However, when researchers immersed a dozen frogs in an open pot of cold water on a stove and gradually increased the heat, they found a different response. The uncomfortable frogs, never sensing that their lives were in jeopardy, all boiled to death. The increase in heat was gradual enough never to alarm them of the danger.

Suffering Is Optional

The experiment described above reminds me of the saying, "In life, pain is required; suffering is optional." Many of us choose the dangerous option of ignoring our pain and therefore do not heed its warning signal. The result is that we accept unhappiness and suffering as our lot in life. During my recovery, I realized this resignation could be deadly for people as well as for frogs, and I set out to discover why I had stayed in hot water for so long.

Dr. Bernie Siegel wrote about the peril of living "lives of quiet desperation." In his 1986 book, *Love, Medicine and Miracles*, he cited research by Dr. William Morton of the University of Oregon which found the cancer rate for housewives was 54% higher than the general population, and 157% higher than women who worked outside the home.

> When these results were first published, it was assumed there was a carcinogen in the kitchen, and much fruitless research was spent looking for it....However, salaried domestics have less cancer than housewives, despite working in two kitchens....

Little thought had been given to the possibility that the housewives' high risk of cancer could be due to their feeling trapped. Often, these women expressed feeling "cut off from the fuller life" they wanted because they chose to follow the path others indicated they *should* be living. Their seemingly small daily suffering cumulatively led to a potentially deadly disease.

It is not that one lifestyle choice is better or worse than another. While the above research may have uncovered some stay-at-home Moms who wanted to work, a 1994 survey of 800 women by author Liz Curtis Higgs discovered that 30% of working women surveyed wanted to stay at home full time.

The one thing the studies do agree on is that the healthiest and happiest individuals follow their hearts. My recipe is:

Hearken to your heart,
Go with your gut,
and Face your fears.

Definition of Stress:
When your heart is in one place, and your body is in another.
Anonymous

When asked to list their daily activities under a *should* or *want* column, most men and women find their lives filled with *shoulds*. These are the same individuals whose stress levels are higher, and whose health is poorer than their peers. "But isn't pursuit of happiness selfish?" I am asked repeatedly.

No.

Selfishness is often defined as "showing care only for oneself." Now ask yourself: Are the people you have met who have nothing to give to others the happy ones? Hardly. Believing on some level that they are too broken to have anything to give, unhappy people themselves off from life, and dig a hole of self-pity so deep they can't see the beauty around or within them.

On the contrary, the happiest individuals know they have something to give, give it, reap more from the giving, become happier, and continue the cycle.

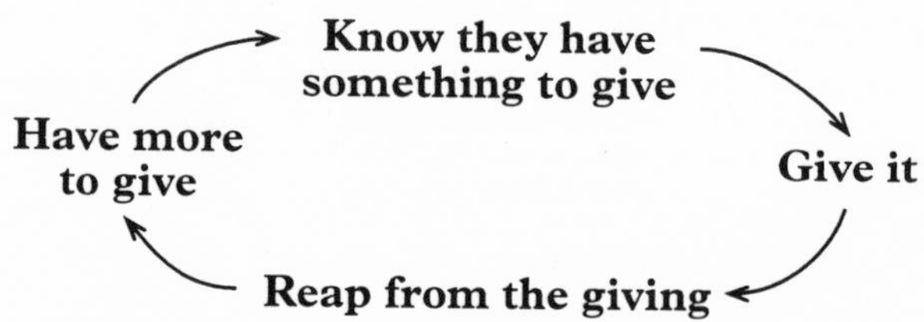

It is the happiest individuals who know the abundance of life and live with great, generous abandon, taking risks and pursuing their dreams of a better world. I ask parents, **"What do you want for your children?"** Always, their reply is **"Happiness."**

Speaking to a group of us in health and wellness careers, Dr. Deepak Chopra, a noted physician and best-selling author, addressed the happiness question head-on.

"What is the greatest cause of death in this country?" he asked.

Most of the audience answered, "Heart disease."

"Cardio-vascular disease, yes. And what is the greatest cause of cardiovascular disease?"

"Stress," we replied.

"It is unhappiness. If you are happy, you are safe. If you are not, you must go find what gives you joy....The greatest number of heart attacks occur on Monday mornings between the hours of seven and nine, to people driving to jobs they do not enjoy."

Later that evening he asked us, "Why do you in America work so hard?"

We chuckled as a gentleman answered, "To have money!"

"And why do you want this money?" Chopra continued.

To which the man's response was, "To buy things!"

"And why do you want to buy things?"

"To be...happier."

"Why not be happy first? Then everything else will follow."

We have all heard,
"Whatsoever you do to the least of my brethren...."
But what if the least of my brethren is me?
Carl Jung

Taking care of our needs and regular self-nurturing are definitely not selfish pursuits. These must come before nurturing others, not because they are more important, but because we must do first things first.

For example, it is not more important to stop and put gas in my car than it is to drive my kids to school. But if I don't do the first, I may not be able to do the second. Taking care of yourself and finding personal joy in life is part of every person's life mission. As author and lecturer Stephen Covey notes, "We must 'sharpen the saw' before we tackle the woodpile of the day."

Living with the goal of making others happy is as frustrating as it is fruitless. Once I looked back over my adult life, I could see that my acting like a doormat was only training others to wipe their shoes on me. Neither I, nor the person who "uses" me in this manner, comes away feeling good about it.

The Golden Rule:
Do unto others as you would have them do unto you.

The Silver Rule:
Do for yourself at least as much as you do for others.

The Iron Rule:
Don't do for others what they can do for themselves.

While in the domestic violence shelter, I did a lot of writing. During my journaling one evening, I realized I had to make a decision. Since my people-pleasing was not pleasing people, I decided one person was going to be pleased and happy with who I was each day. And that person had to be me.

Wanting To Be Liked

Years later, a businesswoman approached me after one of my seminars. "I know I have a strong desire to be liked," she began. "Is there anything I can do about it?"

"There's nothing wrong with wanting to be liked," I replied. "But tell me, have you ever liked someone you did not respect?"

She couldn't say she had.

I reminded her that respect must come first. Only then can the liking follow. Respect comes from having the personal integrity to stand up for our own opinions, needs and values. Constantly taking care of others in a way that depletes yourself only ends in bitterness, regret, and a "you-owe-me" mentality. It is a lose-lose situation for both the giver and receiver. In order to spread happiness, we must first have it. In order to have it, we must be true to ourselves.

------------------------ **EXERCISE** ------------------------

Question:
By becoming more myself,
following more of my dreams,
asking for what I needed,
and setting limits on my time and energy expenditure,
did I lose a couple of friends?
(Answer on bottom of next page)

The Most Loving Choice

When I finally understood what the counselor had meant when she said "No adult victims, only volunteers," I realized personal happiness was within my reach. I also saw that being happy was the most loving thing I could do for myself, as well as for those around me. I began my search to learn how to accept life's most wonderful gift.

I soon realized, like Dorothy in *The Wizard of Oz*, that what I was seeking had always been within me. I just needed to remind myself that the witches and demons could be melted once I exercised my God-given wisdom and power.

The Attraction Factor

I am often asked if "No victims, only volunteers" means we *create* all the negatives in our lives? No. I do believe, however, that we *attract* either negative or positive experiences. This was made painfully clear to me when I began dating again at age 36.

It was two years after my divorce, and I realized I had very few men friends. I decided, somewhat reluctantly, to join a video dating service.

The first time I got a call from the service telling me I had been selected by a gentleman, I went into their office to see the video of his interview. As I watched, I felt nothing positive or negative, so I went up to the desk and said, "I guess I can meet him for lunch."

At this point, the owner walked over and asked, "Oh, who selected you?" When she saw his name she said, "I don't believe it! Over 500 men and you've attracted the only alcoholic in the service!"

"I didn't attract him! He selected me!" I said, trying to defend myself. She simply replied she was not going to allow me to go out with him. She later put a note in his chart stating, "Sometimes Pete drinks too much."

On my next visit to my counselor, I asked her if I had actually attracted the problem drinker. She told me that I could be in a room of 1,000 healthy men, and the least healthy one would find me and ask me out. Her good news was that as I learned to be healthier, I would attract healthier relationships.

Children *can* be victims. "No victims, only volunteers" would never apply, for example, to child abuse. But adults who stay in abusive relationships are in a prison inside their own heads, with bars created by their beliefs about themselves and life in general. Once these are unlocked, (the goal of our next section) they are free.

Finally, I must add that I believe that sometimes we allow painful circumstances to come into our lives because, on some level, we know that the lessons we will learn from the experience will be worth the pain. Life teaches lessons through our challenges. Therefore, our job is not to blame others or ourselves but to focus on understanding the lesson to be learned.

Learning The Lesson The Hard Way

The Oct. 29, 1995, cover story in *Parade* magazine recounted

Answer: Yes, but did I lose a couple of *friends*? Or just a couple of inaccurate assessments!?!

the lessons Captain Scott O'Grady learned after being shot down behind enemy lines in Bosnia. His stories of eating leaves and insects to survive, illustrate how he handled living in constant fear and deprivation for six days.

The article heading included this quote: "With death at my front door, I found my key to life." Later in the article, O'Grady said, "I underwent a rebirth....My time in Bosnia was completely positive....I felt the most incredible freedom....I knew I'd never be lost again."

Today Captain O'Grady speaks around the country of his gratitude for the lessons of his experiences.

When I teach my ***Taking Care of Me*** program in shelters, I remind those in transition: "Every painful experience in life can either make you bitter or better." Pain can make us better only if we learn the lesson it has to teach us.

There is a purpose for every challenge
and every situation in which we find ourselves.
The purpose is for learning and growth,
and for getting to know who we really are.

Karol Kuhn Truman,
author of *Feelings Buried Alive Never Die*

Some years ago, I came across Cherie Carter-Scott's list of "Rules for Being Human." The first four rules challenge us thus:

1. You will be given a body.
2. You will learn lessons.
3. There are no mistakes, only lessons.
4. Every lesson will be repeated until learned.

Television talk-show host Oprah Winfrey once said, "First, life gives you a pebble, and you don't get it. You get a brick, you still don't get it. Then, you get a brick wall. If you still don't get it, then, you get an earthquake, and the whole house falls down on your head."

While this is true, we don't have to live the "No pain, No gain" slogan. Not all lessons have to be learned under extreme or painful conditions. Some can be learned by listening to a grand-parent, watching a flower grow, or reading a book.

Unfortunately, for those of us too stubborn to believe it until we see it, we must often learn the harder way.

Once we accept that there are no mistakes, only lessons, we feel more in control of our lives. The shelter was the worst and the best thing that could have ever happened to me. Because it was the worst, I learned my lesson well.

Simple, But Not Easy

You have begun the most exciting change of all: becoming more fully who you are. It is the journey of integrity.

Throughout this book, you will feel yourself being pulled closer and closer to congruity between what you know to be true and what you live. We either live the truth today or we have to face the truth tomorrow.

To thine own self be true,
and it follows that
thou canst not be false to any man.
William Shakespeare

As your guide for this part of the journey, I promise that the steps you will learn here are simple, but not always easy. If some of these life-changing concepts seem too simplistic, let me remind you of the wisdom of Glenda, The Good Witch, in *The Wizard of Oz*.

When Glenda appears to show Dorothy how to go home, she simply shares her heel-tapping instructions with the phrase "There's no place like home."

Hearing this, the Scarecrow is indignant. "Wait a minute!" he challenges. "If it was that simple, why didn't you tell her before?"

Glenda responds with her all-knowing smile, "Because she

wouldn't have believed me."

We often must walk life's yellow brick road before we understand the simple lessons at the end.

Changing our mind and opening our heart is simple, but not easy. This program requires honesty on a very deep level, and that can be painful. Another of my favorite wizard stories is from the cartoon series by Johnny Hart, creator of *The Wizard of Id* cartoons.

In this particular strip, Rodney, the cowardly knight, goes to the Wizard's cellar to request a favor. Rodney explains that he is preparing to go into battle the next day and needs something to make him courageous and strong. The Wizard tells him to have a seat, turns to his cupboard, and pulls out a three-foot hypodermic syringe. When he turns back to the knight, Rodney has run away.

Once we realize that pain is required, but suffering is optional, we have new courage to face temporary discomfort for the benefits of a long-term outcome.

The Most Important Question

As I shared earlier, on my first day in the shelter, my final question to the counselor was: "Why would anyone run from happiness and choose misery and chaos?"

We will hear some answers in the next chapter, but before we do, take a moment to imagine this scenario:

EXERCISE

A courier is due to arrive at your front door any minute with a beautifully wrapped package containing Abundant Happiness. The package has your name on it. Why might some people in this situation be tempted to run out the back door?

Jot down three or four answers to this question and put them aside before continuing.

The greatest discovery of my generation
is that human beings,
by changing the inner attitudes of their minds,
can change the outer aspects of their lives.
Written by philosopher William James in the year 1897

In Pursuit Of Happiness

First, let's define happiness. We aren't talking here about a giddy school-girl-crush kind of feeling. Happiness is not the euphoria of falling in love, constantly feeling up, living a stress-free lifestyle, or the absence of sads and mads. Rather, happiness is an attitude which is much larger than any individual emotion. Others have named it peace, joy, hope, love, gratitude. We'll just call it happiness.

My stay at the shelter helped me realize that I had been choosing to run from happiness most of my adult life. Now, after speaking with thousands of adults, I realize most of us unconsciously turn down happiness. Why would we do such a thing?

Over the past five years, I have addressed this exact question to hundreds of different economic, gender, and ethnic groups. When asked, "Why do people run from happiness?" each group gave me the same four basic responses. Compare your answers with theirs:

THE FOUR REASONS WE RUN FROM HAPPINESS:

___X___1. Fear Of Getting It

_______2. Fear Of Losing It

_______3. The Belief That We Don't Deserve It

_______4. Guilt

#1: Fear Of Getting It

This fear is also phrased as "fear of change," "fear of the unknown," or "fear of success." Certainly, greater happiness brings change. Will happiness mean we have to change careers or our group of friends? Not necessarily, but if our pursuit of happiness entails such changes, we will *want* to make them when the time comes.

I'll never forget the gentleman at my first corporate seminar who blurted out, "Hey, if I were really happy, what would I talk about at break?" He feared, as many of us do, that happiness was boring.

Is Happiness Boring?

I remember growing up thinking nice guys were boring, stable jobs were boring, and healthy foods were boring. The concept that happiness and excitement are mutually exclusive is perhaps best promoted by the soap operas, with their dozen new crises each program. Does anyone on these programs look happy? In real life, happiness is even more exciting than chaos.

Richard Bach, author of *Jonathan Livingston Seagull*, once wrote, "We are never given a dream without the power to make it come true." Today, knowing I can achieve anything I can conceive, my life is far from dull. Dozens of times in the past few years I followed my heart, and it has always given me a lot of exciting things to talk about at break!

A Dream Come True

I recall wanting an interview with best-selling author Nathaniel Branden in Los Angeles. I had read many of his books, and his tape-set, *The Psychology of High Self-Esteem*, really opened my eyes. I wanted to interview him before starting my national speaking, but I wasn't sure where the $500 airfare to Los Angeles would come from, since most of my income went back into supporting my new business. Nevertheless, I believed I was given this dream, and with it, the power to make it come true.

First, I called Dr. Branden, who graciously consented to be interviewed if I could come out that August. That day, I began talking to my friends about how exciting it was going to be to meet him. The next Sunday, after the service where I direct a gospel choir, my pastor asked if I would consider taking a trip. He had heard a wonderful Catholic gospel choir in Los Angeles, and wanted me to experience it for myself. "Of course, the parish will pay your airfare in gratitude for all you have done," he added.

Thrilled, I told him that would be great.

I then called the church in Los Angeles to make sure the St. Brigid's choir was singing on Sundays in August. After the secretary assured me they were, she and I chatted about my trip. Then she asked, "Would you like to stay in our guest house?"

I told her that would be super!

I was able to hear the choir, meet the beautiful people of St. Brigid's, interview one of my all-time heroes, and visit Universal studios - all in the same weekend!

No crisis on a soap opera can compare with the excitement of following our dreams.

Suffering is what human beings do best.
What takes real courage is to be happy.
Nathaniel Branden

The Four-Letter Word For The Key To Happiness

When best-selling author Sid Simon gave a workshop at Creighton University in the late '70s, he referred to a study conducted by two psychotherapists. This couple's year-long sabbatical was spent interviewing the happiest people they could find in 33 different countries.

Their research found that an individual's level of happiness is determined largely by a four-letter word. Any guesses?

The word is not "Cash," "Time," or even "Love." They noted that many people all over the world who had an abundance of love from other people were still miserable.

The therapists' research clearly indicated that the four-letter word for the key to happiness was "**Risk**." Over the past seven years, I have discovered how true this is. Love and joy come to those who risk. Risk-takers do not second-guess themselves with "What if?" questions. They live life more deliberately. They usually do not achieve immediate popularity, but they do know the supreme happiness of living with integrity.

At this writing, the top box-office hit of all time is about such a character, Forrest Gump. Why have we responded so positively to this simple film? Because it is the story of a man who is loving and happy. It is also about a man who is an incredible risk-taker.

One of my favorite scenes has Forrest running across the country because he "feels like it." At first dismissed as crazy, he is soon lauded as a folk-hero, and hundreds of people decide to run with him. Then one day, he stops and goes home, leaving his followers to find their own path.

A new idea is first condemned as ridiculous
and then dismissed as trivial, until finally,
it becomes what everybody knows.
William James

The Greatest Risk

Forrest Gump reminds us of the greatest risk we can take at any given moment: to be ourselves and speak our own truth. I realized in the shelter that I had spent my entire adult life trying desperately to please my parents, my bosses, my students, the Church, my boyfriends, and eventually, my husband. Nowhere had I truly succeeded.

During that time, I was also unable to enjoy compliments or let good feelings in. My people-pleasing efforts had resulted in my becoming a chameleon. Therefore, when people complimented me, since no one had ever seen the *real* me, I concluded that they were merely complimenting the aspect of me I had created to please them.

When I accepted my painful failure to make others happy, I released a large amount of guilt and fear. As I began to be more self-comfortable and authentic, love grew. First, I experienced greater self-love. I embraced myself with all my strengths and shortcomings. Then came the love of those who accepted and celebrated the person I truly was. The friends I kept, after putting them through the "fire" of my new, more real selfhood, turned to gold.

Today, the quality of my relationships surpasses any I previously had. My friends are the women and men who are drawn to me, and I to them, because we are great risk-takers.

------------------------- EXERCISE -------------------------

1) **Reflect on a risk you've taken that you're glad you did.**
2) **Now ask yourself: What are three risks I'd like to take, but haven't yet?**
3) **Describe what is keeping you from taking each of these risks.**
4) **Discuss your insights with a friend or counselor.**

The Coward And The Hero

Did you ever consider who has more fear, the coward or the hero? If you think about it, you'll realize both have the same amount. The difference is that the coward uses the fear as an excuse to stay stuck, while the hero feels the fear and takes the risk anyway. The hero's mindset is one of "What have I got to lose?" This allows them to take public, private, and personal risks.

Public Risks

What does a public risk look like? These are the times we stand up to others "out in public" for what we believe. Some examples of public risks in my own life include:

- Writing a letter to the editor of my Catholic university newspaper about the lack of a campus ministry center. The day after the paper came out, I received a phone call from the university president with an offer to let me select a house out of the four they had available for renovation.

- Adding a drummer, a bass player, and a sax player to our Catholic church choir long before others in our area had done so. It quadrupled the attendance at that liturgy within two years.
- Interrupting a gentleman at a town hall meeting who was rattling on about "bombing the Commies," with, "Excuse me, but have you ever *met* a Russian citizen?" I doubt that it changed his mind, but he did end his diatribe.

The number of public risks I've taken that did *not* end so well are numerous. I remember taking a Sunday choir job at a Presbyterian church during my college days. It was "just a job" where I walked in, put on my choir robe, and sang my solo. I didn't even know anyone's name other than the choir director's.

It was the eighth or ninth such Sunday, and the preacher was slamming his fist on the pulpit as he shouted warnings to us about the hell-fires awaiting sinners. Suddenly, something inside me snapped.

"Pastor," I interrupted, my heart pounding as I stood facing the astonished congregation. "We have heard we are sinners for the past three weeks. We have heard about hell for the past three weeks. When are we going to hear the *good* news, that we are forgiven and loved?"

At that point, I ran out of the church (leaving the choir robe at the door) never to return again. The pastor called me later that week to thank me for my candor. He said coffee and rolls after church developed into a most "invigorating discussion." But despite his invitation, I never went back. I simply could not face those people again after my judgmental words.

Personal Risks

Personal risks are the one-on-ones. They include those times you tell a friend that something she said hurt you, or you really appreciate him and haven't ever expressed it. Some personal risks in my life include:

- Asking John Rosemond, author of six books on parenting,

if I could be part of his national team one minute after introducing myself at his seminar. He later offered me a speaking contract.
- Walking up and introducing myself to Senator Bob Kerrey, who had run for President of the United States the previous year. I then mentioned to him that since it was 12:30 on a Sunday afternoon and he was in his jeans, I could tell he hadn't been to church yet. He smiled and said, "I meant to go." We chatted, and he began attending our service the following week.

Just Do It.
Nike advertising slogan

Be not afraid.
Jesus Christ

My greatest personal risk was the Thanksgiving Day my family will never forget. I walked up to the television we were all watching, turned it off, and stood in front of it. "Are we going to talk about the fact that I was in a shelter, or is this one more secret we are going to sweep under the rug and pretend never happened?"

After they recovered from their shock, we began a discussion/debate that concluded with prayers and hugs five hours later.

The Test Of A Real Friend

The personal risks I've taken that did not end well are etched in my mind. They have been relatively few in number, very painful, and extremely enlightening. The one I recall most vividly involved two of my best friends.

At a party in my honor, I introduced my two good friends to each another, knowing they shared many interests. They hit it off immediately. Soon afterwards, they decided to build me a gift for my upcoming wedding. It would be a surprise! The result was that they and their significant others met two nights a week, leaving little time for outings I could be included in.

When the wedding week arrived, I received their beautiful bookcase with great joy. Since the project was finished, I could now have my friends back! But they continued to make plans without including me or us, and I felt more and more isolated.

One day, about a month after the wedding, one of my friends was walking into choir practice at the same time I was. I asked her if we could speak a moment in private. We slipped into a chapel and sat down. As I began to share with her that I felt like I'd lost my two best friends, the tears began to flow. "I'm sorry," I said as I wept. "I didn't mean to cry." I reached down in my purse to get out a tissue, and when I looked up, she was standing at the door.

"I have to go. Rehearsal is about to start."

That was the last thing she said to me for many years. She did not return my call the next day or my letter the following week. The other friend had a completely opposite response when I spoke to her. She embraced me, apologized, and invited me over shortly thereafter.

One friendship was strengthened by the truth of my pain. The other was destroyed. But about situations like this, I like to remind myself: I didn't lose a friend, just an inaccurate assessment.

Private Risks

Finally, there are those private risks in the solitude of our lives where we come face-to-face with the mirror of who we really are. Whether it's taking the risk to journal, to pray, to cry, or to admit a wrongdoing, these can be life's greatest risks. Here, only *we* can ignore our needs and return to our old ways.

My greatest personal risks have been confronting my binge-eating, confronting my co-dependency, and choosing to protect my health and happiness by separation and divorce.

We have met the enemy, and it is us.

Walt Kelly's Cartoon Character, Pogo

Because of the work I do, hardly a week goes by that I don't meet someone who has demonstrated tremendous courage in facing their personal demons.

Just last week I met a couple who shared an amazing story. Both were divorced when they met. Previously, he had admitted to a sexual addiction and sought counseling for it. After they were married, she chose to face her workaholism, leave her 65-hour-a-week management position, and go home to raise her one-year-old. As I listened, I heard great joy and pride in the fact that they were preparing to celebrate their tenth wedding anniversary.

A thief who faces his or her dishonesty, an alcoholic who stops drinking, a depressed parent who seeks counseling, a teen who admits an eating disorder, an employee who leaves a good job to start his own business: Each is an example of how we can take a personal risk back to integrity and wholeness. These are life's unsung heroes.

Am I Fully Alive?

Risks don't always turn out as we had hoped, but they always bring greater insight and the reward of living every day to the fullest. When my daughter was in the third grade, she came home one day from science class with an exciting insight. "Mom, do you know how you can tell if a plant is alive?"

"How?" I asked.

"If it's growing!"

I told her that is the same way you can tell if a person is alive. To be fully alive, we must take risks.

Life Without Risk

When I was still in my 20s, my single aunt was twice my age, but we would often socialize together. One day, when I called to invite her to an outing, she informed me she was through with such things. "Don't ask me to any more singles' activities," she said. "I'm done with all that. I give up! I just want to stay home and be by myself."

A year later on her fiftieth birthday, I was at her hospital bedside when the doctor told her she was full of inoperable cancer.

When the chaplain on call at the hospital that day walked into her room, his first question to her was, "Are you recently divorced or widowed?"

"I've never been married," she said through her tears.

"And how do you feel about that?"

"I've been bitter about it most of my life," she admitted.

"Let's start there."

Could her "giving up" have increased her susceptibility to a disease such as cancer?

Isolation is the darkroom where I develop my negatives.
Anonymous

Dr. Bernie Siegel reminds us that we must continue our personal growth, or we may find ourselves one day with a physical "growth." Part of this journey to wholeness is the risk of connecting with others.

We all face the challenge of living every day to the full. In our search for greater happiness, fear and despair are the great enemies. We decide each day to move toward or away from life. The most urgent question for us is not, "Is there life after death?" but rather, "Is there life *before* death?"

Security is mostly a superstition.
Avoiding danger is no safer in the long run
than outright exposure. Life is either
a daring adventure or nothing.
Helen Keller

THE FOUR REASONS WE RUN FROM HAPPINESS:

________1. Fear Of Getting It

___X__2. Fear Of Losing It

________3. The Belief That We Don't Deserve It

________4. Guilt

#2: Fear Of Losing It

Let me assert my firm belief that the only thing we have to fear is fear itself.
Franklin D. Roosevelt

"If I got it, I'm afraid I might lose it!" is a popular excuse for not pursuing greater happiness. We can lose many things. The stock market could crash. Our home could be leveled by a tornado. The person we love might leave us. However, our level of happiness is not determined by having things or relationships. Happiness is a state of mind. We cannot have happiness taken from us; we can only choose, consciously or unconsciously, to give it away.

When we choose to let our fear of tomorrow's loss destroy our serenity today, what are we saying? "Since I might be devastated a month from next Thursday, I'll just start being depressed today. Then when it comes, there's no big surprise." How much sense does that make?

A Story Of Self-Sabotage

"I think I'm destroying something good because the pain of losing it would be more than I could bear." This amazing statement was uttered to me one evening by a beautiful 22-year-old. I asked her to explain.

She recounted that every Friday night for the past month her new boyfriend had driven an hour from his home to take her out. The week after she started my class, they were on their way to a restaurant when they had the following conversation:

"Boy, you sure smell good," she commented.

"Thanks," he said.

"I thought you came here right from work."

"I did."

"You wear cologne to work?" she asked.

He nodded. "A little. I put on extra for you."

"I've never known a guy to wear cologne to work. Do you

have somebody on the side?"

At this point, he turned to her and said, "No, I've got three on the side. I've been meaning to tell you."

"You're playing with my mind!" she retorted.

"No," he replied. "You are. Could you figure out why?"

She went on to explain that he was the most wonderful man she'd ever dated, and how terrified she was of losing him. Once she recognized her underlying fear of loss and how it was affecting her, she was able to work on her own esteem and make changes that allowed the relationship to flourish.

This young woman's story is common. We hate to be disappointed. Somehow we believe that if we expect the worst and are wrong, we'll have less pain than if we expect the best and are let down. We'll do almost anything to avoid the risk of hitting Rock-Bottom.

Fear Of Rock-Bottom

Rock-Bottom is the mental state many of us landed in the night of our first big heartbreak, or the day we missed out on a big job opportunity. Rock-Bottom is the dark night of the soul. Its darkness comes not from the circumstances, but from the lies we choose to believe.

There are two beliefs that make Rock-Bottom so dangerous:

1) We believe nothing we can ever do will improve our present situation or relieve our intense pain.
2) We believe no one has ever felt this way before, and therefore, we choose not to talk to others about it. We believe, "They just wouldn't understand."

These are two of life's greatest lies, and most of us will face them at some time during our lives. Therefore, it is crucial that we remind ourselves of these truths:

1) The light at the end of tunnel is always there, but sometimes, because we're going around a curve, we just can't see it.
2) Our pain is not unique to us. Everything we are facing has been faced before. We will all face Rock-Bottom thinking at some point in our lives.

The Secrets We Keep

One of my Rock-Bottoms occurred while my parents were out one evening. I was 11 and had never heard about menstruation. My first period began while they were gone, and I thought I was dying in a terribly degrading way. I told the sitter not to bother me and went into my parents' bedroom. I laid down in the middle of their bed and arranged my hair to look nice (just in case I died before they got home).

When my parents returned four hours later, Mom came in, sat on the edge of the bed, and asked me what was wrong.

I told her of my impending doom, and she smiled as she apologized for not telling me the facts of life sooner. (I formally forgave her when I was 23.)

Although I can smile, too, as I recount this story today, it reminds me of the serious responsibility we have to accept the facts of our physical and emotional lives. Rock-Bottom is as much a part of growing up as any biological function. Pre-teens or teens who commit suicide are often those who don't make it through their first dark night of the soul. By letting our secrets out of the closet we will strengthen our families and ourselves.

The Lesson At The Bottom

A few years ago, a man in his 40s came into my office and said, "I want to be just like you!"

I assumed he didn't mean he wanted small ear lobes and fat knees, so I asked him what he meant.

"I want to be a high self-esteem person!" he exclaimed.

"Sorry," I said, "I don't fill the bill. Just ask my kids about my low self-esteem days. But I can help you have more high self-esteem days. I call them 'A-Days.'"

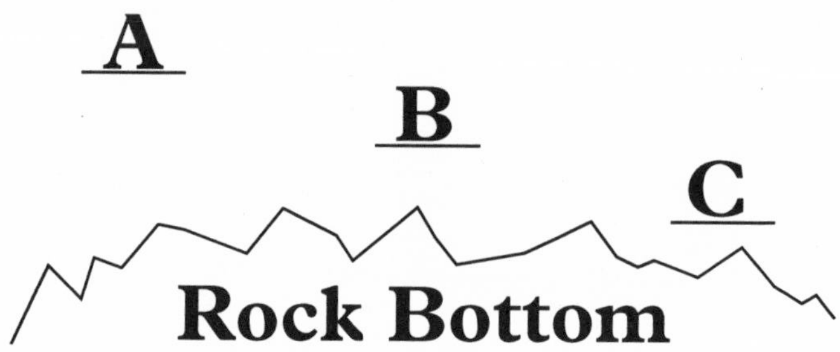

A-Days occur when we feel on top of the world; we're at our best and expecting the best of those around us. But occasionally we have B-Days where little things go wrong, like a bad-hair day or a non-matching-socks day. Then we can have C-Days. The car dies. The fish dies. The relationship dies. Our hope dies.

When I am confronted by someone who is miserable, having weeks or months of C-Days, I remind him or her that taking risks is the only way to get from a C-Day to a B or A-Day. The gentleman in my office, realizing he was living a C-Day life, looked perturbed. "No way!" he said. "Taking risks is how I ended up this low!" I could just see him building his little condo at C-level.

"But you're miserable!" I protested.

"You got that right," he said. "But this is my comfort zone." It was his *uncomfortable* comfort zone. I reminded him that he really had nothing to lose by taking a risk. The most dangerous place for us is really level C. (Remember the frogs in the pot of water?)

The fear of taking one more risk may be considerable, but if we succeed, we're up to level B. If we fail, our pain from hitting the rocks will be so great it will overshadow our fear of taking risks. We'll take the action needed and find ourselves at level A once again.

When I was in the shelter, I didn't sit and ask, "Should I take a risk and change my life? I just can't decide." On the contrary, the decision was one of the easiest I've ever made. The pain I'd been experiencing was too intense to do otherwise.

EXERCISE

Reflect back on some of the happiest people you have known. Write down four or five names. Now ask yourself:

- **What do they have in common?**
- **Are these people who have been through some hardship, such as a death or near-death of a loved one, or overcoming an addiction?**
- **Are they people who have great money, fame or power?**

Determine your own recipe for happiness and discuss your findings with a friend.

In the past, my fear of loss of happiness resulted in extreme insecurity that often brought about the negative event I most wanted to avoid. Whether it was in a relationship or in an audition for an acting role, I was often my own greatest saboteur. When I booked my first national speaking engagement, I recognized this fear and was able to face it head on.

Author John Rosemond had just invited me to be one of three speakers for his Center for Affirmative Parenting. His letter read, "I love your stuff! Let's go change the world together!" I was ecstatic, on a hope-filled "high."

Shortly thereafter, Rosemond called to inform me that my first audience would be "one of the toughest" - a Young President's Organization chapter. (YPO's are presidents of multi-million dollar businesses by the time they are forty.) I was to speak to this YPO assembly on a cruise ship off the coast of California. In four hours of presenting to them, I would make or break my young career as a national speaker.

After Rosemond's call, I neither ate nor slept as I wrestled with my fear of losing his respect and embarrassing myself in front of the YPOs. Then I remembered the story of the two millionaires.

A Fable Of Fortune

In a small Midwest town, there were two next-door neighbors, Harry and Ernie, who each headed successful million-dollar businesses. Harry had inherited his flourishing business from his father. Ernie had started his from scratch.

In the midst of their success, along came a stock market crash. Instantly, both men lost everything. Their friends and neighbors were very worried. To have lost so much! How would they handle it? Finally, a small group of friends got together to visit the men and see how each was faring. One former millionaire was - as they had feared - devastated. The other, however, was just fine and as determined as ever to rebuild. Who was devastated? Harry, who had inherited the fortune, or Ernie, who had earned it?

Of course, the devastated man was Harry. He felt he was a *victim* of luck - both good and bad - and was therefore disheartened by his loss. Ernie, on the other hand, knew he was the *inventor* of good fortune. He knew what is known by all the world's happiest individuals: My greatest asset for achieving happiness is myself, with all my God-given talents and abilities. No one and no circumstance can take away this most precious resource.

So, how did my talk aboard the cruise ship go? Superbly. Why? I took not only my gifts with me, but also Eleanor Roosevelt's reminder: "No one can make you feel inferior without your consent." Once I realized I could walk off the ship with everything I had when I walked onto it, (plus an additional good tan) I released the majority of my fear and anxiety.

Many of us stay stuck in suffering because we fear the pain of loss. We must realize that pain is our friend.

The Gift Of Pain

I recall a woman in her 50s who described herself as "miserable." Her source of pain, in her words, was that her husband didn't love her. I asked her if she knew that for a fact, or was only surmising it to be true. "Oh, I could never ask him," she replied. "I'd be too afraid of the answer."

Had this woman summoned the courage to ask, she might have been pleasantly surprised. Even if her husband had said, "No, I don't love you," her pain would have set her free. How? Either by allowing her to let go of wondering about his affection, or through igniting her anger and energizing her to take positive action.

Did you know there is a physical disease in which those afflicted have no pain? If it sounds like that wouldn't be so bad, think again. The disease is leprosy.

I learned about leprosy on a television show aired during the '80s: *Magnum P.I.*, a series about the adventures of a single-guy private detective on a Hawaiian island.

In one particular episode, Magnum's new girlfriend had a health problem. As the two of them walked along the beach barefooted, she revealed that she had leprosy. Slowly the camera panned down to their feet as they approached a sharp, rusty, metal object protruding from the sand. Viewers watched as she unknowingly impaled her foot on the object, oblivious to the pain or the danger she faced.

Playfully, she then challenged Magnum to a race to the water. Splashing around in the ocean washed away any evidence of the injury. After a commercial, the program resumed with a somber scene. Magnum and a physician stood by the young woman's hospital bedside. "I'm afraid we didn't catch the infection in time to save her foot," the doctor said. "We'll have to amputate."

Lack of pain was the cause of the young woman's misfortune. Pain, whether physical or emotional, is every person's friend. But you wouldn't guess it from listening to TV commercials. "Get rid of your pain with PAIN-NO-MORE," the ads seem to scream. This is a dangerous mindset.

Imagine reacting to a fire alarm, for example, by simply turning it off while the fire rages on. Yet when we take a pain-killer, we usually turn off that warning without investigating the source of the problem.

EXERCISE

The next time you have physical pain, take a moment to thank your body for the stress indicator.

Then, rather than distancing yourself from the pain, ("I wish I could cut off my head!") focus on it for a few seconds, breathing into that place in your body and visualizing it expanding and relaxing.

The results will amaze you.

Just Say 'Yes'

We tell our youth, "Just say 'No' to drugs." A much more powerful and appropriate message would be "Just say 'Yes' to feeling and respecting your pain." Words are not enough, however. Young people need to not only hear this message, but see us honoring our pain for bearing important news that something, somewhere in our lives, is not right.

I have heard dozens of stories over the years about the extraordinary lengths we go to in order to avoid pain. One that stands out in particular occurred in a small non-profit corporation. The secretary of this business had, over the course of a year, embezzled over $12,000 from the business to "help out" her boyfriend.

Although there were many warning signs that this activity was occurring, the small staff chose to avoid facing the pain of confrontation, in hopes the problem was not real or would somehow take care of itself. The staff rescued her as she had rescued her boyfriend, until the problem reached the crisis stage. At that point, her behaviors came to light, she was fired, and the company was forced to move to a smaller office in order to survive.

This scenario is a common one. We get ourselves into messes not only because we are afraid of the painful changes in *our* lives, but we often go to great lengths to rescue *others* from the pain of reality and growth as well.

The Results Of Rescuing

I once saw an excellent example of the ill-effects of rescuing on the popular television talk-show, *Oprah*. I had just finished listening to the premier performance of Maya Angelou's poem for Clinton's inauguration, when Ms. Winfrey's program came on.

She was interviewing three mothers who had repeatedly loaned money to their adult children despite the lack of payments in return. One mother had a son in college who had borrowed money for such items as a boat, a truck, ski equipment, and jewelry for his girlfriend.

Another mother had repeatedly loaned money to her 25-year-old son and was now suing him to get it back. Oprah pointed out, "You don't all of a sudden get to be 25, and you're irresponsible. I'm sure, as his mother, you have seen signs all through his adolescence that he was irresponsible. So why would you make a loan to somebody who is irresponsible?"

"If we hadn't loaned him the money the second time, he may have gone to jail," replied the mother.

"You should have let him go to jail," challenged an audience member. Instead of facing the immediate pain of a few days behind bars, the young man was suffering through humiliation in front of millions of television viewers.

Rescuing people from the natural consequences of their behavior never helps. When we rescue others from pain, the result is always worse than the pain we were attempting to help them avoid. Tough love of a child is difficult but necessary. In the past, many parents used the excuse, "We can't afford it," to keep balance in family life. Today this is often just not true. Parents must simply say, "No."

Time For Tough Love

A woman called me a few months ago to see if I knew of any good career counselors for her daughter. "How old is your daughter?" I asked.

"Twenty-six."

Without asking any further questions I stated, "She's living at home with you and pays no room or board."

"Of course she can't pay us room and board, she has no job," said the mother.

"Since you called to ask for my assistance, here's the most helpful thing I can tell you: Charge her $25 per month for room and board starting the first of next month, then double it every month until she moves out. If she can't pay and won't move out, put her belongings in the driveway. If after 24 hours they're still there, call Goodwill to pick them up. Any questions?"

She couldn't think of any.

Whether avoiding pain in our own lives or working to protect others from pain, our efforts often backfire. But we can choose at any moment to run toward happiness rather than to continue running away from the danger of loss.

I believe the concept of loss is an inaccurate assessment. Change is not loss. In my belief system, every good thing that is "lost" is simply exchanged for another good thing. Even death is not life-threatening.

Whatever your belief system, what you believe will determine what you fear. It will also determine your level of happiness. Although few of us ever completely overcome our fears, the more we are able to move toward this goal, the more we will relax into the natural and powerful flow of health and happiness.

I keep the telephone of my mind open to peace,
harmony, health, love, and abundance.
Then whenever doubt, anxiety, or fear try to call me,
they keep getting a busy signal,
and soon they'll forget my number.
Edith Armstrong

THE FOUR REASONS WE RUN FROM HAPPINESS:

________1. Fear of Getting It

________2. Fear of Losing It

____X___3. The Belief That We Don't Deserve It

________4. Guilt

#3: The Belief That We Don't Deserve It.

This is the most common reason we avoid happiness and often the most difficult thinking pattern to transform. Therefore, as we begin to see through this fallacy, the truth has tremendous healing power.

------------------------ **EXERCISE** ------------------------

Imagine you are addressing 500 high school students tomorrow. You are asked to speak on the topic, "How to deserve happiness."

- **What will you say?**
- **How long will you speak?**

To be happy, do we have to be free from flaws, 99 and 44 one-hundredths percent pure, like the old Ivory Soap commercials used to claim? Since such perfection is unattainable, such a belief would condemn us to a life of misery. Would we require such standards of our children before we allowed them the right to happiness?

Hardly.

There are only two possible answers to the question of who deserves happiness:

1) We all have a birthright to happiness by our very existence. (Even the American Constitution says so!)

OR

2) No one deserves happiness. It is a free gift. We must simply open up our arms to embrace it.

It sounds so simple, yet still we resist. Most of us want to recite a litany of reasons why we are not deserving. For one person, the reason is a disastrous mistake made years ago. For another, it's something bad that's been done to him or her. For a third, it's a compilation of all the little mistakes made in life that builds a mountain of unworthiness. We can distort and magnify our brokenness to the point of paralysis.

Jane's Story

A good friend of mine, I'll call her Jane, was very unhappy in her marriage. When Jane discovered her husband's repeated unfaithfulness, she decided to take her young son and move from California back home to Iowa.

Suddenly, the husband's mistresses didn't look so good to him.

Cards and letters, flowers and gifts began arriving at Jane's home daily. But none of these received a warm response, including the final telegram that read, "I cannot live without you." Three days later, she received a call saying her ex-husband had attempted suicide.

In Jane's mind, this was her ultimate reason for not deserving happiness. She had taken a vow to love and honor her mate "till death do us part," and now she felt responsible for almost ending his life.

Her owning responsibility for his action had serious negative effects. A year later, Jane's smoking had increased. Meanwhile, her weight had decreased to the point where her family practically forced her into a retreat weekend for separated and divorced individuals. Jane reluctantly agreed to go.

When she arrived at the retreat site, Jane was horrified to discover that her small group leader was a minister. She recalls thinking, "Don't these people know God doesn't care for my kind?" She had reached her Rock-Bottom.

During the first small group discussion, the clergyman asked the woman seated next to Jane to share something about herself with the group. The woman began, "Five years ago, my ex-husband attempted suicide, and I've never really been able to forgive myself since."

Jane started to reach out to reassure the woman that it was not her fault. As she did, she watched in amazement as everyone, including the minister, reached out as well. Witnessing this outpouring of love for someone in her own situation, Jane began to cry uncontrollably. Her tears broke the dam of self-reproach that had held her prisoner all those months.

With the help of the weekend retreat, Jane was able to forgive herself and gently close the door on her past. Today, she is happily remarried.

We all live with the objective of being happy;
our lives are all different and yet the same.
Anne Frank

Who Is "Self-centered?"

Someone once asked me if my classes on self-esteem and self-empowerment puffed everyone up and made them think they were better than anyone else. I responded that I had met only one person who seemed to think he was better than everyone. It was a man who was adamant that everyone know he had the IQ of a genius. He was also a homeless alcoholic.

On the other hand, I meet people nearly every day who think they are worse than everyone else. It is this group of individuals that fits my definition of self-centered. These individuals give very little to others, because they believe they have nothing to give. Their fixation with their own feelings of inadequacy, fear, and guilt consumes the time and energy they could use to share their gifts with the world.

As long as we believe our brokenness is the greatest, we are caught in a web of suffering that prevents us from moving on with life. A good phrase for all of us might be, "My pain is ordinary." Such a belief would help us live *extraordinary* lives.

Bad things happen to everyone. If we do not let the wounds heal, their memory may fester within us for years. As a result, there are often disastrous results of hanging on to a victim mindset.

------------------------ **EXERCISE** ------------------------

Suppose that three days ago you fell down and scraped your forearm badly. Now you are with a group of friends and are describing how awful the wound looked. You only have a scab now, and it just doesn't do justice to your story, so you finally pull back the scab to show your friends the original wound.

- **What would be the long-term effects of such an action if repeated over time?**
- **Have you known people who reopen their emotional wounds week after week or year after year?**
- **What are the effects of these actions?**

We often fall into a victim thinking pattern without realizing it. We reopen old wounds to talk about them "one more time." But just as the body cannot heal this way, if inner wounds are constantly reopened, emotional and spiritual healing are inhibited. The "infection" caused from continually reopening old wounds often causes a festering that is worse than the original problem.

We have all made mistakes and been the recipient of others' mistakes. Forgiveness is not forgetting. It is accepting that *we were all doing the best we could at the time with the information we had.* Forgiveness of yesterday is necessary to attain real freedom and joy today.

During my time at the shelter, I realized I had never forgiven myself for being imperfect. I had a mental list of all the things I wanted to "fix" about myself. Once I realized the list was never going to diminish in size, I had a new decision to make:

1) I could continue to berate myself and hold back self-acceptance until I was "fixed," creating more misery and self-deprecation for the rest of my life,

OR

2) I could accept that I was a broken vessel, and learn to love and honor myself despite my cracks and chips.

I chose the latter. Shortly thereafter, I realized that the only way that I could stop trying to fix me was to envision myself as "un-fixable." That is why I created a new paradigm and resolved to start seeing myself as: Half-Jerk/Half-Jewel.

Half-Jerk/Half-Jewel

As I started to become comfortable with this concept, I realized there were two important rules included in it:

1) The ratio would never change, no matter how hard I tried to improve myself. It would always be 50/50.
2) Everyone was exactly the same as I was at their core.

This paradigm shift altered me, freed me. I relaxed. I became more honest about my shortcomings, accepted compliments more graciously, stopped looking down on myself or up to other people. I forgave myself. I became aware that those around me were just as broken and blessed as I.

This helped me become more loving, more patient, and less prone to compare myself with others. No matter how handsome or beautiful, intelligent or powerful others looked to me, I now knew there was a jerk lurking within who needed healing and love just as I did. And no matter how despicably cruel and selfish another might appear to be, I now knew there was a jewel waiting to be discovered and cherished.

---------------------------- **EXERCISE** ----------------------------

Before you continue, take a moment to complete this phrase one to three times: "I'd be happier if only...."

All answers to the above sentence completion fall into one of two categories.

1) Something impossible to change, such as, "...if I were taller," or "...if I had different parents."

OR

2) A bad habit or characteristic which *can* be changed, such as, "...if I had more time," or "...if I stopped procrastinating."

Changing What I Can

In the second category, change occurs when we find out why we are hanging onto the problem. I use Nathaniel Branden's "The good thing about..." sentence completion exercise detailed in his book, *The Art of Self-Discovery.* We each can look within to know why we hang onto problems such as: too busy, too poor, or too overweight.

When I asked **"What is the good thing about..."** to individuals facing a challenging habit or situation, they answered:

CHALLENGE	THE GOOD THING ABOUT IT IS:
...having no free time?	I don't have to deal with my problems/feelings/memories.
...not having lots of money?	I won't become greedy or immoral.
...not losing weight?	Not having to deal with all that attention from the opposite sex.
...procrastinating?	It's a rush! And people aren't disappointed if it's not perfect when I wait until the last minute. They're just glad to get it!

When we unstick our thinking, desired results soon follow.

Accepting What I Cannot Change

The above sentence completion exercise works wonders for those challenges we can change. To understand the harder-to-change category of "if onlys," it is necessary to refer back to the Half-Jerk/Half-Jewel concept. When I ask teenage girls to complete the "I'd be happier if only..." phrase, they most often respond with, "If only I were prettier!"

"I believe every gift in our life has an inherent shortcoming," I challenge them. "What might be a drawback of being stunningly beautiful? The more beauty I have, the less I'd have of what other gift?"

It sometimes takes the girls a minute, but usually their consensus is "personality." I tend to agree. Beautiful women have an obvious and wonderful gift, but they usually aren't the best at making new friends. They may not need to, because as soon as they walk into a room, people are drawn to them.

How about the ability to tell a joke? Do we expect to see a Miss America contest where five of the ten finalists do stand-up comedy routines? It is highly unlikely, as they've never had to learn to hold someone's interest by being a comedian. They hold it by their loveliness.

Another good example of the Half-Jerk/Half-Jewel concept is the tendency towards right-brain or left-brain dominance. The more right-brained we are, the more creative and spontaneous we tend to be. The more we function out of our left-brain, the more organized and analytical we will probably be. It is a continuum:

Left_______X________________________________X_______Right

You can be here or here

but you cannot be both places. Every time we move closer to one end, we lose out in the other category. As a strong right-brained person, I tend to be messier and nonchalant about being ten minutes late for a lunch date. Yet on a good day, I can write a talk, an article, and a song.

Do I want to trade places with my more left-brained secretary? No! Does she want to trade places with me? Never! Nor would either of us want to give up some of our gift area in order to be precisely in the middle. Individuals in the middle are often just as content where they are, grateful for their unique gift of balance. We each have different gifts and different weaknesses, but they all add up to an equally whole person. (Note: "Whole" is where the word "Holy" came from.)

What about extremely intelligent individuals? Early in my speaking career, I met Steve, a freshman in high school. He came up to me after one of my talks to ask a question. "I'm the smartest in my class," he said, sincerely concerned. "What is my weakness?"

While Steve and I went for a walk, I told him I appreciated his openness. "Let's look at the gifts of people whom the world calls 'slow'," I suggested.

We came up with examples, such as a Down's syndrome child. We could see that such children often have big, loving hearts, are non-judgemental, laugh more easily, and have more patience. "Do you lack any of these gifts?" I asked him.

"I'm very impatient. And sometimes quite critical. That's it!" he concluded. Then he thanked me and left.

If only we were all so willing to face our shortcomings!

------------------------ EXERCISE ------------------------

- **What is something in yourself you can't change but would like to?**
- **Ask friends or family members to help you find a gift in this "brokenness."**

--

Not Wanting To Be Nosey

Most of my life, the thorn in my side was the nose on my face. I hated it from the first time I saw it in a three-way mirror when I was twelve. I truly thought God had made a mistake. So you can imagine how I felt twenty years later when I was offered a chance to fix the "un-fixable."

I was having dinner with my sister and her new boyfriend, who happened to be one of the top plastic surgeons in the country. Just as we began our dessert, he paused and leaned over to say, "I could do great things with that nose of yours." He was even going to give me a discount!

I seriously considered the offer for a few seconds before responding with, "I'm kind of attached to it, but thanks!"

At the time, I wasn't sure why I turned down such an opportunity, but about a year later, that reason revealed itself. A gentleman walked up to me after a service at our church and said,

"Your solo was beautiful today, Mary Kay. You get down on your knees every night and thank God for that nose!"

I looked at him in shock. "What are you talking about?"

"You understand the resonance the shape of your nose gives, don't you? Didn't it ever occur to you why Barbra Streisand didn't get a nose job?"

It never had.

My voice is one of the gifts I am most grateful for. I truly cannot imagine life if I couldn't sing to comfort myself, to praise God, or to wake my kids up in the morning. And to think I almost ruined my gift because it was attached to a "weakness."

I now see that no matter what characteristics we manifest, there are equal benefits to each:

- Introversion and extraversion,
- Being a feelings person or a thinker,
- Being a big-picture person or a detail fanatic.

Each gift is important and beautiful in its own way.

No one is less strong than another.
Every person can do one thing better
than any other 10,000 people.
Donald Clifton and Paula Nelson,
authors of *Soar With Your Strengths*

Specially Gifted

At the Seattle Special Olympics a few years ago, nine young contestants lined up for the 100-yard dash. Adrenaline coursing through their bodies, the runners took their starting positions. At the gun, all took off, except one boy whose cleats got caught in the starting block, causing him to fall. When he cried out in pain, all eight of the other runners ran back to help him. The cheering for all of those winners continued for over 10 minutes.

The Virtue Of Humility

How does the Half-Jerk/Half-Jewel theory fit in with striving for humility? It is my contention that this is the only formula that permits healthy humility.

If you believe you are less than Half-Jewel, you are judging yourself too harshly and comparing yourself negatively to those around you. Once you have done this to yourself, it is a short step to judging others. True humility is not the belief that you are worse than someone, but that you are no better than anyone. The only way to come to the latter conclusion is to accept that we are all equal in both gifts and brokenness.

I have never seen a greater monster
or miracle in the world than myself.
Montaigne

So why don't we all act out our brokenness to the same degree? Because some of us accept it. Surprisingly, the key to abating the negative within us is not to like it, but to own it. Nathaniel Branden once wrote, "What we resist, persists."

By the same token, the negatives we accept diminish.

------------------------- EXERCISE -------------------------

The Saints and Monsters Exercise

1. **Think of someone you admire. Choose someone who is (or was) a person in your life, rather than someone you have merely read about. Write down two or three of their admirable qualities.**
2. **Next, think of someone who drives you up a wall or gets under your skin. Write down two or three of the most irritating qualities in this individual.**

Judge Not

If the Half-Jerk/Half-Jewel formula is true, then how do we so readily put some people on pedestals and others in the dungeon?

This is due to a process psychologists call projection.

Mental health professionals identified projection just a few decades ago, but it is based on the age-old wisdom that what we admire and despise most in others is also found in ourselves to some degree. We project our denied faults and gifts onto the "screen" of this other person, thereby enlarging what is there to the level of monster (negative traits) or saint (positive traits).

The greatest of all faults is to be conscious of none.
Thomas Carlyle

For example, everyone is a tad bit irresponsible and dishonest. When we can accept that in ourselves, rather than project it onto "enemies," we become more responsible and more honest. Mother Teresa is humble, yet she is the first to thank God for her gifts. She is humble because she owns her weaknesses. True humility is staying aware of our own brokenness and refraining from judging the brokenness of others.

This does not imply that every time we judge an action as wrong, we have imitated it. However, when we hang onto some characteristic that bothers us in someone over a long period of time, we are usually expending a lot of energy despising a purely human weakness. The reason for this is our own lack of self-acceptance in this area.

Many Aboriginal tribes have a ritual at each full moon. Gathered around an evening campfire, they look across their circle to the person opposite them to become aware of whatever they admire most and judge most about that person. Then they look within to accept those positive and negative qualities in themselves.

At whatever point you judge another person,
it is you who do the very same thing.
Romans 2: 2

Different gifts are the spice of life. We need not envy others for what we do not have, for we have a gift they do not. Each of our gifts carries with it a corresponding shortcoming, and each of our weaknesses holds a balancing strength. Once we realize this, self-comfortableness sets in and joy is close at hand.

------------------------- EXERCISE -------------------------

To counteract the almost universal belief that we do not deserve happiness, write or share aloud your thoughts about the following:

- **Imagine your best friend sending you a letter confessing everything terrible he or she has ever been a victim of or done. The amazing coincidence is that this is exactly what has happened to you in your life. At the end of the letter, your friend begs forgiveness and asks if you are still willing to be friends.**
- **Will you deny your friend happiness or love as a result of his or her shortcomings?**
- **Do people have to be perfect to be happy?**

I am as good as the best.
Walt Whitman

In Review

To find happiness, we must release these two enemies: fear and judgement. We have discussed the first two reasons we run from happiness:

1) We fear getting it.
2) We fear losing it.

We have seen that these fears are inaccurate assessments.

3) We judge ourselves unworthy.

We have seen that this judgement is inaccurate as well.

The fourth and final reason we run from happiness includes both fear (of scarcity) and judgement (of self). We must now face our shame.

THE FOUR REASONS WE RUN FROM HAPPINESS:

________1. Fear of Getting It

________2. Fear of Losing It

________3. The Belief That We Don't Deserve It

____X___4. Guilt

#4: Guilt

True guilt is guilt at the obligation one owes to oneself to be oneself.
R.D. Laing, British Psychiatrist

This final reason we run from happiness makes as little logical sense as the first three, yet it is also extremely common. Just the other day, a young woman came up to me after a seminar and bemoaned, "If I were really happy, I wouldn't feel like my mother's daughter!"

Ever heard the phrase, "If Momma ain't happy, ain't nobody happy?" It is a wonderful reminder that unhappiness and misery are contagious. Why then, do we often feel guilty about being happy?

A God Who Loves Suffering

I find a large part of the answer in the teachings of certain religious groups. As a Catholic, for example, I was taught to give up whatever I liked best during Lent so I could grow in holiness. Although there are definite benefits to abstinence, the result for me was that I looked for ways each Lent to increase my pain level. In fourth grade, my girlfriend and I jumped barefooted on the rocks behind school in near freezing temperatures to be "holier." I had concluded that God loved suffering.

This belief lingers for others today. A man I'll call Ben went to see a priest a few years back because he had fallen in love with a young Catholic woman and wanted to know about her faith. In a 15-minute interview, one of the priest's axioms was, "And if you are too happy, you are not doing God's will." Fortunately, this is not a teaching of the Catholic church, but one man's misguided interpretation.

Recently, while working with another priest to prepare a Lenten television program, I heard him rephrase the concept of Lenten sacrifice beautifully for our audience. "This year, my friends, don't give up something that makes you happy. Give up something that makes you sad."

Guilt over happiness and, "If it feels good, it's bad" thinking are not limited to Catholics. Everywhere I go, I run into people who still believe such notions.

The Story Of The Guilty Son

I remember the day a very excited gentleman wearing a three-piece suit walked into one of my seminars. "I'm so glad I finally get to take this class!" he said as I welcomed him.

"Great!" I said. "What has kept you from attending before now?"

"I just wasn't ready. But today I registered at the university to begin my graduate classes. I'm going to get my master's degree in social work."

"What *have* you been doing?" I asked.

"Law. Hated it for years. But Mom always wanted an attorney, and I had the grades, and since I was the youngest of four sons...Well, once you get the degree, you feel like you gotta use it."

"So what was it that helped you to finally follow your dream after all these years?"

"Oh, Mom passed away about six months ago."

As parents, we often unwittingly pressure our children to live out our dreams to "make something of themselves." The message we send to them is often, "I want you to be happy. I want so much for you to be happy, I'm going to make myself miserable just so you can be happy." Thus, the child grows up with two very mixed messages. Our talk says, "I want you to be happy," while our walk says, "The most loving thing I can do for you is to be miserable for your sake."

If each generation gives up its own happiness for the sake of its children, who is ever happy? No one. Therefore, in my talks to parents, I give them the most challenging homework they could possibly have: **"The most loving thing you can do for those you love is to be happy."**

Obviously, there must be a balance, but I find that many more parents err on the side of living their lives through their kids, with no personal goals of their own. This creates an over-indulged child and an under-indulged parent.

EXERCISE

If there was such a creature as an over-indulged child or an under-indulged adult, what would one look like? Make a list for each of the two categories.

Over-Indulged Children

I asked a group of parents and teachers to list characteristics of what over-indulged children and under-indulged parents look like. Their list was as follows:

OVER-INDULGED CHILD	UNDER-INDULGED ADULT
Bored, mouthy, ungrateful, belligerent, dressed perfectly, nervous, unhappy and susceptible to depression.	Exhausted, tense, resentful, often sick, nervous and unhappy, often depressed.

Sound like someone you know? Certainly this imbalance is not good for either the child or the adult. It is the adult's responsibility to maintain a balance between caring for his or her own needs and those of the children.

Are You "Guilty?"

With guilt as our guide, we can find numerous excuses to run from happiness. Here are three of the most common:

1) **All or Nothing Thinking:**
"I care about people, so I will never be happy until they're happy." This is a prescription for world-wide misery. The poor will always be among us, as will those addicted to drugs, gambling, food, and complaining. Joining the ranks of the miserable in the name of guilt-ridden love is a most *unloving* decision, since we will

simply spread what we most want to avoid!

2) **Loyalty To Those Without:**
"He sold out," is a remark I hear every once in awhile from inner city teens. They are referring to those who have become financially successful. Such individuals are sometimes labeled and ostracized, as though their achievements are somehow disloyal to the community from which they came.

A young woman came up after a presentation I'd given and shared, "I've been living in poverty for years. I'm a single parent, and that's what my family expected of me. Now I realize my affluence will in no way be harmful to them. In fact, I can be a model of where we all can go." (She became an instructor for me a few months later and started sharing her wonderful message.)

3) **Belief In Scarcity:**
We often believe, "If I don't suffer, someone else will have to." This infers that there is only so much happiness to go around. It's called scarcity thinking. I used to believe there were only so many good men out there, so I got jealous every time a friend found one. I also believed there were only so many nice homes, good jobs, or beautiful summer days. I was constantly worried about loss or competition. When I stopped worrying, my life changed.

Financial Freedom

One of my insights into how guilt pervaded my thinking occurred as I dealt with mental ruts about financial success. I realized early in my business career that I had a habit of sabotaging my financial success whenever it started looking too promising. After all, during the late '60s I'd marched in Washington, D.C., carrying banners with messages about the evils of money and power.

To get beyond this limiting mindset, I pulled out Dr. Branden's exercise for exposing subconscious agendas and wrote, "The good thing about making less money is...." I was amazed as

I continued to write, "...then no more children will starve in India." I was shocked, hardly believing I had written those words that were obviously buried deep inside me.

My particular "button" for this happiness issue was my belief that there wasn't enough money to go around and that my having more would cause increased suffering in the world. Instant Guilt!

To get out of the guilty mentality, I had to create a new picture in my mind: A paradigm of abundance. By recalling that one out of every 100 people in this country is a millionaire, I reframed the situation. My extra income would come from all those millionaires' pocket change! I determined they would never miss it, and no one would have to suffer because of the abundance I acquired. As a result, the money I was ready to receive poured into my life.

The Inaccurate Assessment

A gentleman at one of my seminars asked this question, "I'm stuck at an income of $40,000. I feel like I've hit my own glass ceiling. Could I have a hidden agenda?"

I asked him to tell me every association he had with the number $40,000. "It's how much my Dad made," he told me. Within minutes we identified his inaccurate assessments about "How much you make is how much you're worth."

Once he separated his Dad's value from his Dad's income, he could continue to honor the former while surpassing the latter. He was able to free his thinking and break open his "ceiling" almost immediately.

Being happy is the most loving thing you will ever do for those you live with or work with. It's that simple. I asked a group at a large corporation to write down ten things they could do to improve their attitudes at work. Before starting to write, one woman yelled out, "I could quit!"

The man across the aisle from her said, "Now that would improve everyone's attitude!" Laughter broke out. Happiness and misery are both contagious.

Before we leave this subject, we need to ask: Is guilt ever appropriate? I believe there is one form of guilt that is. When I have a moral value and I step outside of it, I feel uncomfortable and guilty. I appreciate the nudge this guilt gives me to get back on track with my values. All other guilt is, in my view, inappropriate, especially guilt about being happy!

Contagious Misery

Let me conclude this section about guilt with a story of a 19-year-old GED student who came to me for help. "I don't know how to stay positive," he began. "It's easy at school, but when I get home, my Mom's always reminding me what a loser I am. Like yesterday, I forgot to take out the garbage, and she said that she was tired of throwing away all her time and money on somebody so worthless.....What am I supposed to do with that?"

First, I reminded him of his need to protect himself against such poisonous, destructive criticism. He agreed and said he knew he needed to move out. Then I assured him that he was not the object of his mother's hatred. "Oh, I know it's herself she hates," he said. "She tells me about every other day she wishes she were dead."

This mother's misery was draining the joy from the life of her beloved son. Unhappiness is not only contagious, it's deadly.

The Truth Sets Us Free

We have all avoided happiness in one way or another throughout our lives. Therefore, in addition to acknowledging the four falsehoods in this chapter, we need to counter them with truths. Our affirmations might look like this:

1) Counteracting the fear of getting greater happiness:
   I am no longer afraid of greater happiness or the changes it will bring. Rather, I welcome happiness with all the new adventures that accompany it.
2) Counteracting the fear of losing happiness once we have it:
   I cannot lose happiness. I am safe. Since I choose not to give anyone or any event the power to take my happiness and serenity from me, I know that happiness is mine each day that I choose it. When what seems to be a loss occurs, I remember that the most important things in life have no end, and that the road to success is never a straight line.

3) Counteracting the belief that we do not deserve it:
Each day that I live, I remind myself of my worth and the worth of all living beings. Understanding that we are all Half-Jerk/Half-Jewel, I will honor my own gifts, own my weaknesses, and not put anyone above or beneath me. I know that happiness is a free gift that, rather than having to deserve, I may choose to invite into my life at any given time.

4) Counteracting the feelings of guilt:
I know there is abundant happiness. By being happy, I am spreading happiness to those with whom I live, socialize, and work. This benefits myself and all those around me.

We all live with the objective of being happy;
our lives are all different and yet the same.
Anne Frank

It is easy to see how we can and must change our minds and choices. Healing begins within, and it begins with letting the light of our joy, beauty, talents, and power shine forth.

This truth is reflected brilliantly in the words of South African President, Nelson Mandela:

> ***It is our light, not our darkness, that most frightens us. We ask ourselves, who am I to be brilliant, gorgeous, talented, and fabulous? Actually, who are you not to be? Your playing small doesn't serve the world. There is nothing enlightened about shrinking so that other people won't feel insecure around you. As we let our own light shine, we unconsciously give other people permission to do the same. As we are liberated from our fear, our presence automatically liberates others.***

President Mandela's Inauguration Speech, 1994

Wisdom is knowing what to do.
Skill is knowing how to do it.
Thomas Jefferson

Once we accept that happiness is not only good for us but good for the world, we can begin the process of determining what we could do immediately to be happier and healthier. How do we sum up happiness? The happiest, healthiest, and most successful people use the term "attitude."

The Attitude Factor

"He's got a great attitude!" or "Her attitude is lousy," are comments often heard in the workplace. So what is attitude? Webster's Dictionary defines it as a "state of mind." I prefer to describe it as *our core set of beliefs and the resulting behaviors.*

Our core beliefs are either positive/hopeful or negative/hopeless. Likewise, our attitude is either positive or negative. Most likely, you've never heard anyone's attitude described as "neutral." The basic belief of a positive attitude is the premise of this book: "We have the power to take control of our lives." This concept empowers us and helps us get out of victim thinking.

We can picture it this way:
Negative Attitudes are B.C. = Blaming and Complaining
(giving away our power)

Positive Attitudes are A.D. = Acting and Dreaming
(owning our power)

B.C. personalities are hooked into the past and what has been done.

A.D. personalities are fully in the present with a clear and optimistic view of the potential of the future.

For example, one young woman I knew was extremely critical of men and could often be heard blaming the entire gender for the problems of the world. One day she was especially upset about men "sizing up women's bodies." After she calmed down a bit, I asked her if she liked her body. She admitted she did not. When we looked at what she could do to start feeling better about herself and her appearance, her hope returned, and her attitude improved greatly.

Positive Attitude is not a set of feelings. One can feel sad or mad, but still retain hope and a positive mentality. Meanwhile, more positive attitudes tend to be found in those who have a flexible rather than a rigid range of emotions. Negative attitudes are often lurking beneath either a pasted on frown or smile. Both can be dangerous to our happiness and health.

So, does a positive attitude create happiness? Or does happiness create a positive attitude? For our discussion, we will assume both to be true. The good news is that although most of us feel less in control of our level of happiness, we can easily understand how our attitude is in our control. It is the result of the choices we make each day.

------------------------ EXERCISE ------------------------

Using a percentage from 0 to 100, how important do you think Attitude is for:

- **obtaining wealth?**
- **recovering health?**
- **success in general?**

--

At my first national speaking engagement, I began my talk by asking 30 CEOs of multi-million dollar corporations how important they believed attitude to be in achieving financial success. Their answer? 95%!

Years later in Dallas, I asked a group of over 1,000 nurses and nursing managers how important attitude was for healing. 95% was their consensus!

Ask any sports professional how important attitude is to winning a competition, and the most successful will tell you, "110%!"

Our attitude is within our control. Once we have changed our thinking from Victim to Volunteer, there are numerous behaviors that will improve our attitudes and our level of happiness from day-to-day.

Surprisingly, it's often the simple little things that make the big differences. Once we are away from, "If only I won the lottery," victim thinking which gives power to those outside of us, we can begin to use our own power to change our attitude.

------------------------ EXERCISE ------------------------

Imagine that today you received news that your workplace had changed its salary scale for the coming year. Starting next week, everyone will be paid, not by their skill level, education, or years of service, but based on their attitude for that week, as recorded by the "attitude detectors" throughout the worksite.

The individuals with the most positive attitudes will get "split-the-lottery" kinds of bonuses, while those with the most negative attitudes will get minimum wage with no benefits. Those in-between will receive salaries and benefits commensurate with their attitudes.

Now, write out your answers to the following:

1) **What would you do differently to earn the highest income? (list 20 or more things before continuing)**
2) **What will keep others from earning a high salary?**
3) **Who at your workplace will most likely start out at the highest salary? Why? Describe their behaviors.**

After you complete the previous exercise, check back to the answers you gave to question #1 and ask: "How many of these behaviors take more than five minutes a day or cost more than $10 a week?" Usually it is very few. The attitude adjustments which we push to the end of our to-do list require neither time nor money. They only require commitment.

A positive attitude is not the result of magic fairy dust sprinkled on us at birth. It is the result of specific day-to-day behaviors. Positive attitudes occur in people who engage in positive, proactive behaviors. For example, 30-year-old Brenda who felt stuck in her job could:

- Journal her affirmations and dreams every day, then
- Begin to feel energized and empowered, then
- Take a risk and apply for a better job, then
- Get that job or
- Decide to keep her old one, and do it with greater dedication.

No matter how positive or negative our attitude is at this moment, we can improve it with the proactive behaviors listed in the upcoming section. Taking the mystery out of attitude adjustment is one more step on the road to successful living.

Attitude Adjusters

The following list of positive attitude promoters is offered in alphabetical order for easy reference. It is not meant to be a comprehensive list, but rather a list of factors that make the most noticeable and long-term differences.

Keep in mind that no one behavior is a magic key. All behaviors are ingredients. Some very positive people might only practice one or two of these behaviors on a regular basis. Others mix three to five in any given week. Your recipe for success will be unique to you. Find what interests and motivates you from the list, then make a commitment to do it.

The Top Twelve Happiness Habits:

Ask for what you want.

Be here now.

Change your self-talk.

Dream and set goals.

Expect the best.

Feel all your feelings.

Gratitude and giving.

Hugs and touch.

Insulate against negativity.

Journal.

Keep on keeping on.

Lighten up and laugh.

The Survival Game

I recently spoke with a gentleman in the Air Force who described his first session of survival training this way:

> We were herded into a room and told we were just captured behind enemy lines. Then we were asked to name the one thing we needed most for survival. We guessed canteens, compasses, matches, pocket knives, you name it. When we were done, our commanding officer said, 'You're all wrong. It's PMA! Don't ever forget that the most important thing keeping you alive is your Positive Mental Attitude!'

Attitude helps us not only survive, but thrive. Therefore, our primary question each day must be, "Is my attitude today one of love, joy, gratitude, and hope?" Until it is, we can neither find happiness, nor spread it.

What you and I will become in the end
will be just more and more
of what we are deciding and trying to be right now.

John Powell, S.J.
author of *Through Seasons in the Heart*

Habit A: Ask For What You Want

Ask and it shall be given.
Matthew 7:7

She was a beautiful woman in her mid-thirties. Her eyes were red from weeping as she walked toward me. After everyone else left the session, she shared how a recent trip to Florida with her husband rekindled her yearning to live near water. However, due to his job, they had lived in the Midwest for ten years.

"I stood on the boardwalk, crying like a baby. My husband reached out to me, but I just gasped, 'I'm dying...we're dying...I've got to move back...I can't take it anymore.'"

I asked her how he responded. "He said he had noticed how peaceful I seemed there. That he hadn't seen me this happy since the last time we were in Florida."

Her husband saw that her request was not only a matter of preference, but a deeply felt need. When they returned home, they began working out a plan to get the family back to the coast.

She then shared how she had been afraid to ask for what she needed for fear it would inconvenience her family. Now she realized her efforts to be unselfish could have destroyed her health and her marriage.

By letting those around us know what we need, we are simply giving them a more complete picture with which to make decisions. Not to do so can be dishonest and, in the long run, destructive.

In his best-selling book on marriage, *Getting the Love You Want*, Harville Hendrix says it is extremely hard to get couples to ask for what they want, so he often asks them what they *don't* want. His advice includes these steps:

1) Identify a complaint.
2) Isolate the desire behind the complaint.
3) List a few do-able behaviors that would satisfy the desire.

These simple steps work not only in a marriage, but in all of life. Just ask yourself: How much of what I don't ask for do I get? Probably not much. Now ask: How much of what I *do* ask for do I get? My life experiences and research indicate that, in time, we will get nearly 90% of what we ask for in a non-aggressive manner. It's a risk worth taking.

So, why don't we just ask? There are many reasons:

1) **We aren't sure what we want.** We need to journal.
2) **We believe our needs aren't valid and believe we don't deserve it.** We must realize we all deserve to have our needs met.
3) **We believe in scarcity: "There's not enough for me to have some."** We need to understand that life offers abundance.
4) **We believe, "If they really cared about me, I wouldn't have to ask."** We need to realize mind-reading doesn't come with management promotions or wedding rings.
5) **We would feel personally rejected if someone told us "No".** We need to realize the answer is about them or about the situation, not a personal affront.
6) **We believe only weak people ask for what they want.** We need to know that the healthiest and most successful people financially, as well as in relationships, are those best at asking for help.
7) **We fear getting it. "What if things still didn't improve?" Or we worry, "What if they *do* improve and I don't have anything to complain about in the break room?"** Here we need to remember that successful people make plenty of mistakes, and break rooms can be transformed from fume-ing rooms to fun rooms.
8) **We don't know how to ask without sounding whiney or belligerent. We're afraid we'll cry or lose our tempers.** We need to learn how to ask.

Good communication occurs when one person receives the

same message the other person sent. Sound easy? It's not. For example, I might be sending a message about two or three different events at once: "I'm upset with you about what you said today, but I'm really still angry about your not following through on your promise yesterday," is communicated as, "You can be so inconsiderate!"

The receiver is then left to unravel all the meanings. What is she referring to? What does she want? Why is she attacking me? If the unraveling looks too arduous, the receiver may simply give up and end the exchange with an attack of their own or by withdrawing.

So how do we avoid the scenario described above? Through a simple but powerful four-step process. This "four-mula" clarifies for both parties what message is being sent, while avoiding judgements and helping us stick to the facts.

At first, the steps may seem awkward or too formal for regular use. However, many variations are possible. I use some form of this formula practically every day. Once you become familiar with the process, you can develop your own style for saying the same thing in different ways.

How To Ask For What You Want:

#1) When___(event)___happened at___(time and place)___

#2) I felt (got)____________________

#3) because____________________

#4) therefore I would like you to consider__________ OR

therefore I am considering____________________

Step # 1: List only one event that happened recently (preferably within 24 hours) with no exaggeration or judgment in your description.

A. **Usual:** "When you *always* leave everything right in front of the door..."
Better: "When you came home from school today and left your books and jacket in front of the door..."

B. **Usual:** "When we *never* go on dates anymore..."
Better: "When it's been over a month since we've been on a date..."

C. **Usual:** "When you said *last week* that you didn't care whether I went on the trip or not..." (not recent enough for you both to remember what was said)
Better: "When you said at lunch today that you didn't care if I went on the trip or not..."

Step #2: State a feeling, not an opinion. Avoid "that", "like", "as if."

A. **Usual:** "I felt *that* you are being rude and careless..."
Better: "I felt really upset and concerned..."

B. **Usual:** "I feel *as if* you don't care anymore..."
Better: "I feel kind of disconnected and isolated..."

C. **Usual:** "I felt *like* you weren't being honest..."
Better: "I got this funny, uncomfortable feeling inside..."

Step #3: Share why you feel as you do <u>without judging</u>.

A. **Usual:** "Because obviously you don't care enough to pick up your things..."
Better: "Because I believe part of my job as your parent is to teach you how to share living space..."

B. **Usual:** "Because you never care enough to..."
Better: "Because our dates are important to me..."

C: **Usual:** "Because you have a tendency to hold things in.."
Better: "Because I wondered if you were still upset about last year's trip..."

Step #4: When appropriate, paint a word-picture of what specific actions could be taken to improve the situation, or warn of a future action you are considering taking if things don't improve.
(It is very important here not to exaggerate, nag, or threaten an action without follow through.)

A. **Usual:** "Don't ever leave things lying around again. I'm warning you!"
Better: "Therefore, if it happens again, I'll simply put the items in a safe, locked place, and you'll have to buy them back for five dollars an item."

B. **Usual:** "If you want this marriage to survive, some things better change!"
Better: "So, I am asking you on a date tomorrow night at seven o'clock. I'll get the sitter. Interested?"

C. **Usual:** "If you're mad about something, you'd better let me know. I can't read your mind!"
Better: "I'd like to take some time tonight, fifteen or twenty minutes, to sit down and discuss the pros and cons. How about right after supper?"

The above steps are powerful and have freed me to feel more comfortable with asking. In addition, when people confront me in a manner which prompts me to feel defensive, I can ask them to rephrase their request using these steps. I can "hear" them much better when this four-mula is used.

EXERCISE

As a novice "Asker," you might want to think of asking for what you want as a game. Simply keep score of the outcome, rather than attaching any great meaning to it. This week use the four-mula to ask for three things from three different people. Record your results. Share them with a friend or counselor.

There are many good reasons to ask for what we want. We feel better, more connected with others. We learn about and validate ourselves by expressing our needs to others. One of the best reasons is that when we get what we ask for, everyone benefits.

The Freshman And The Professor

When I was a freshman at a state university, it was not uncommon to have 500 to 1000 students in each classroom. This severely limited the interaction between students and professors, making it extremely difficult to ask questions. The adverse setting gave me a chance to practice asking for what I wanted.

At one particular lecture, our professor was describing a writer this way; "Of course he believed in God, and we all know *that* is the great delusion."

Something inside me snapped. I raised my hand in the huge lecture hall and was ignored. I stood and waved my hand and was ignored. I finally made my way into the aisle and started down front to where the professor was lecturing.

As I headed toward him, he finally acknowledged me. "Yes, Miss. May I help you?" he asked.

"I hope so, Professor. Will the statement about belief in God as 'the great delusion' be on the exam, or is it just your personal opinion?" After a slight pause, he stated it would not be included on the test.

I believe, as did many of my classmates, that I helped not only myself and my class by expressing my concern, but potentially also the individual I confronted.

Asking for what we want is essential for a balanced and happy life. Like the woman who needed to be near the ocean in the first story of this section, our needs cannot be shoved aside. Not asking for what we want is usually more selfish than asking. Our misery makes others pay a high price for our silence.

There is another important reason we must learn to ask for what we need. Until we learn to ask, we will not trust that our needs will be met. There can be no intimacy without trust. Asking for what we need from another is an important step in building a healthy relationship. Only when we learn to ask will we have the reminders that we are safe and that we are cared for.

What Happens When The Answer Is "No"

It's wonderful that people say "No" to us. It reminds us that we can say "No" as well! My favorite version is, "No, I won't be doing that, but thank you for asking!" Each of us has limits and boundaries and saying "No" is simply admitting that to the other party.

Saying "No" is sometimes more difficult than receiving it as a response. But if we do not say an honest "No" today, the truth of our real feelings will be more painful tomorrow.

Setting Our Limits

Before a recent visit to family members, I called to let them know that I was eating lower-fat foods than last time they had seen me. "So I would appreciate if we could eliminate all comments about what foods I eat or do not eat," I said calmly over the phone.

In the past, such a call might have upset them, but we have all grown. Before other visits, I have requested such things as limits on smoking indoors or the amount of time the television was on. My visits are now more frequent and longer in duration because I have risked making these requests.

Asking is such a simple thing. It not only prevents problems from either beginning or getting worse, it heightens everyone's awareness, so there are fewer guessing games in life.

If No, Let Go

The final step to asking successfully is to let go of the outcome. If we get what we want, that is an obvious good. If we do not get what we want from the other party, we must discern how great our need is, and either go on without or find our needs met elsewhere.

In the examples about my family mentioned above, I can always bring my own food, stay at a hotel, or shorten my stay if visiting becomes unpleasant.

If we have not yet learned to let go of the outcome, chances are we are not receiving honest responses, because people are afraid to tell us the truth.

I have discovered that the asking is often much more important, much more life-giving, than how or when our needs are answered. It doesn't matter whether the answer is "Yes" or "No." When we have communicated our needs in a respectful manner, others have a better understanding of us, and we have a better understanding of them through their response. When the answer is "Yes," which it usually is, we are happier.

When the answer is "No," we are free to make a decision based on truth rather than on speculation. Asking is key to reaching our goals.

If you don't ask, you don't get.

Ghandi

Habit B: Be Here Now

Enjoy today: this is not a dress rehearsal.
Anonymous

The "Be Here Now" habit sounds so simple and so obvious. Where else would I be? And yet the individual in today's society who is living most of his or her life in the present is rare.

There are three distinct skills to living in the present. The first is getting our energy out of the past. The second is getting our energy out of the future. The third is fully experiencing the moment.

Each of us has only so much energy at a given time. When our energy "circuits" are tied up in either the past or the future, we have nothing left for the moment. Thus, we give little to the people and events of today, creating more problems to regret tomorrow.

In Thornton Wilder's play, *Our Town*, the main character, Emily, goes back in time to relive a childhood birthday party only to find presents but no presence. Everyone did things for her, but no one stopped to relate to her, or to be with her. These human beings had fallen into the trap of becoming "human doings." The good news is that we can learn to pull our focus from the past and the future, one thought at a time.

Getting Out Of The Past

Think back to an event where you regret your behavior. Now ask yourself: If I had known *then* what I know *now*, would I have done that? When I pose the question in my workshops, the answer is almost always, "No." Therefore, it's not a matter of your being a bad person then and a good person now. *You did the best you could at the time with the information you had.* So did the other people you have trouble forgiving.

Every time I find myself wallowing in bitterness ("they should have") or regret ("I should have"), I repeat the phrase, "We were all doing the best we could at the time with the information we had." This is extremely freeing. I come back to the here and now. I trust in a Higher Order to take care of any messes made because I believe all things work for good.

One secret of a long and fruitful life is to forgive everybody, everything, every night before you go to bed.
Ann Landers

We can also find ourselves living in the past through nostalgia. The 'good old days' thinking can be another way of keeping our energy frozen in another place and time. But as one friend of mine noted, "Nostalgia ain't what it used to be!"

The majority of individuals with their energy in the past, however, are not reminiscing about the good old days; they are hanging on to regret and bitterness. One woman was so angry about her brother-in-law not repaying an old $300 debt, I felt like writing her a check. But that, of course, would not have resolved "the moral of the thing," that she claimed was holding her back from greater happiness.

------------------------ EXERCISE ------------------------

Use this checklist to determine whether you have been spending your life energy on the past. Then ask yourself how much energy/attention you have given to each.

- **Who have I not forgiven?**
- **What have I not forgiven myself for?**
- **What events am I bitter about from the past?**
- **What embarrassing events still haunt me?**
- **What is my greatest regret?**
- **How much energy am I giving to defending what I have done or said in the past?**
- **How often do I keep score from what happened in the past?**

One high school student I'll call Kathy had lost her boyfriend the previous year in a car accident. One day near the end of our class, she darted out of the room for no apparent reason. At the next class we heard her story.

> It was raining. Not hard, just a light rain. But I was glad. That meant no one else would be at the cemetery. I went to his gravesite. I just stood there crying for a minute, then I said that I had come to take my power back. I promised I'd never forget him, but said I needed to let go and move on. I knew he would have wanted that for me...It felt really cleansing.

That young woman went on to become president of her senior class and continues to amaze me with her wisdom and courage.

Getting Out Of The Future

Living in the future is just as detrimental as living in the past. As mentioned earlier, we have control over less than 2% of what we worry about. Yet worrying has become a national pastime, and is highly accepted in most families, social groupings, and workplaces. When we find ourselves spending mental energy on something in the future, we can think of F.E.A.R. as False Evidence Appearing Real.

My life has been a series of endless crises,
most of which never happened.
Mark Twain

"Be Here Now" does not mean we cannot hope for things to be different in the future. It means we must face what *is* today. This skill is not calling us to a life of instant gratification, but rather to living life one day at a time. We never know when it may be our last.

When I am asked to sing at funerals, I often hear in the eulogy that the deceased was just beginning his retirement years. The minister often notes with regret that what the deceased waited so long for was never realized. We cannot afford to wait until tomorrow to find joy.

How to Be in the Moment

Here is a simple technique to find out if you are living in the present. Sit in front of a blank wall each morning or evening and ask yourself: Where are my thoughts going right now? You will discover that many of them are rehearsing future events. It's good to be prepared. It's not good to be preoccupied.

----------------------- **EXERCISE** -----------------------

Use this checklist to determine whether you have been spending your life energy on the future. Then ask yourself how much energy/attention you have given to each.

- **How much energy am I giving to fears about financial security for myself or my family?**
- **How often do I ask myself, "What will they think if I...?" or "How do I look?"**
- **Do I fear loneliness or losing my close relationships?**
- **To what extent do I feel concern about keeping my job, my clients, or my title?**
- **When do I worry most about "being good enough?"**
- **Do I tend to worry about what a decision will mean for me in the future?**
- **How often do I worry about what will happen to others?**

We do not know what tomorrow brings, but we know what we must do to be fully alive today. Life does not give us a headlight so that we can see the future results of our actions. It gives us a flashlight, so that we can see where we need to take our *next step*. When we do the best we can do one moment at a time, our long-term goals are realized.

Mindfulness And Modern Living

One obvious sign of living in the Now, rather than in the future, is a slower pace and a less driven life style. We do not enjoy anything we rush to get done, yet hurrying is the normal pace in modern society. The antidote to rushing through life is mindfulness, being present to the moment and aware of what is going on within and around us.

Sign seen on retreat center bulletin board:
Things To Do Today: Inhale, Exhale, Inhale, Exhale, etc.

One of my favorite mindfulness memories occurred one evening while I was out of town for a speaking engagement. Since the weather was inclement, my two choices for the evening meal were to go down to the dining room or eat dinner in my hotel room. I strayed from my norm and requested a meal to be delivered to me for the sole purpose of eating mindfully.

When the meal arrived, I quietly sat and took in all of its aroma and beauty. I said a prayer of thanks for those who had grown and prepared the food, as well as to the One who created the growers and preparers. Then I took a bite, and while chewing, focused all my attention on tasting it.

The above paragraph is not great literature, but it was a great meal! I had no conversations, responsibilities, or distractions from the simple and beautiful act of eating. I became painfully aware of how seldom I tasted my food, and wondered if I was more consumed by my daily activities than I was savoring them.

"Sorry, I'm Not Here Right Now"

Many an answering machine recording begins with the above message. It reminds me of the postcard for business-driven executives: "Beautiful scenery. Amazing views. Wish I was here."

A happy and full life demands presence. I remember the time, sitting by a beautiful lake in Colorado, when I heard a car stop suddenly on the rocky road behind me. I looked over to see the driver and his companion jump out just long enough to snap a photograph, then jump back into the car and drive to their next mountain-top experience.

Similarly, I have sung with many accompanists who hurry through their piano solos to get to "the important part" where the singer comes in. As a dancer, my daughter is just now learning the importance of finishing one movement completely before beginning the next.

The shortest way to do many things
is to do only one thing at once.
Samuel Smiles

"Be Here Now" behavior requires us to live each moment as if it were our last. When I feel I am losing this wonder-fullness, I take a deep breath, or meditate, or go barefoot and feel the grass under my feet, or spend an afternoon with a child. I know that if I can become as engrossed in where I am right now as a little one, I can reconnect with bliss, freedom, and the Now.

The wonderful movie, *Hook,* teaches us that if we lose all our todays for the long-term goals of tomorrow, we can forever become hooked into other than our top priorities.

At the 1996 Olympic Games, the father of a silver medalist swimmer who had been coaching his son for 17 years said, "I would love to take him fishing now. It will mean everything to me." Perhaps even more than an Olympic medal.

To Be Here Now:

- Taste your next meal,
- Smell your next flowers,
- Look your loved one in the eye,
- Let your next breath "in-spire" you,
- Hear the next birdsong outside your window,
- Then feel the pillow under your cheek as you lay down to rest.

Habit C: Change Your Self-Talk

Our sub-conscious can't take a joke.
Dr. Bobbie Summers, Ph.D.

What we put into our brains comes out in our lives. Self-talk is a simple, yet powerful way to improve our attitudes for the better. I once heard it put this way:

What we think
determines what we feel,
determines what we do,
determines who we are.

It is crucial that we program our brain-computers for success and happiness. The good news is that programming the brain is simple; no expertise is needed. If we repeat over and over what we want to believe, eventually we will have a "shift" where belief happens. We don't even need to believe what we are saying yet, as we'll see later.

The simplest way to change our self-talk is to learn to replace our "helpless" phrases with "hero" phrases:

Helpless Talk		**Hero Talk**
"I should..."	becomes	"I want..."
"I can't..."	becomes	"I haven't yet..."
"He/She makes me..."	becomes	"I feel____when..."
"That was stupid..."	becomes	"That was interesting..."
"I'll try..."	becomes	"I'll do my best..."
"I am upset/tired..."	becomes	"I feel upset/tired..."

It also helps to avoid "never" and "always," because these are rarely accurate.

I learned about the power of self-talk early in my recovery period. When I first started offering classes in my home, a woman shared, "The holidays are coming, and since I'm going to visit my family, I really *should* lose this weight...."

At this point, the woman next to her interrupted excitedly. She held up the self-talk list above and asked, "Would you like to rephrase that?"

After looking at the sheet, the first woman replied, "Oh, no. I don't *want* to lose the weight!" We were all amazed. After a moment of stunned silence, I asked her what she *did* want to do.

"Well, I'd love to travel."

"So, why don't you travel?" I asked.

"Oh, I've got to lose the weight first."

It was obvious to us that her chances of reaching her weight goal were slim to none because the message she was sending her brain was, "I don't want to lose the weight."

Our Brain-Computer

If you bought a new computer game today and loaded it into your operating system, the first question on the screen might be, "What is your name?" If you typed in your name as "Godzilla," would the computer *believe* you? Absolutely! And so does your brain.

Our brain is a kind of mega-computer that never shuts off. An offhand remark to a friend, such as, "I always get those two phone numbers mixed up," becomes a command/enter to our brain-computer.

Similarly, when we use a phrase like, "I don't want to lose weight," the brain replies with a simple, "No problem." Then it goes about its task of slowing the metabolism or changing our cravings, so that even if we do attempt to diet, we won't find long-term success.

Now, add to this the fact that scientific research has shown that the brain cannot distinguish between an actual experience and an imagined one. It is easy to see why we cannot afford the high price of a negative thought.

If you think you can, or you think you can't, you're right.
Henry Ford

Once when I was teaching my program at a military base, a gentleman threw out the following challenge to the group: "I *should* mow my lawn before inspection tomorrow morning, but I don't *want* to. How will I explain my newfound freedom to my commanding officer?"

I asked him if he *wanted* to live on base. When he answered, "Yes," I reminded him that whenever we make a choice, responsibilities accompany it. He knew the rules when he signed on for base housing. He now had a commitment to keep until he made other arrangements. He agreed to change his self-talk to, "I want to mow my lawn, because I want to live on base."

Once we understand the power of self-talk, we become more aware of the amazing things we have been telling our brains. Recently, I noticed I was sending a negative message whenever my children argued. "I am *tired* of you two fighting!" I would say, and sure enough, I'd need a nap before the day was over. As soon as I started saying, "I want you two to cooperate, or I will separate you," they weren't arguing so much and I wasn't so tired.

The happiness of your life depends upon
the quality of your thoughts.
Marcus Aurelius

The Meaning In The Message

Many people want to discard this formula of feeding our brain more positive messages as too simplistic. During one corporate seminar, I had a participant challenge me with, "This self-talk stuff...I just don't buy it!"

"Do you buy Pepsi?" I asked.

"Of course. What's that got to do with it?" he answered.

I then asked him what three-word national billboard campaign Pepsi was running at the time. "Gotta Have It," he replied.

"Is there any new product information in that slogan about price? Taste? Environmental safety?"

He shook his head. Then I asked him how it was that this campaign was one of the most successful ever used by the billion-dollar corporation. Could it be we are simply giving our computer-brains the message: "(I) gotta have it?" every time we read the billboard?

If you're getting thirsty as you read this, don't be surprised. When Pepsi-Cola's marketing research says the billboard slogan works, chances are it does. Whether with billboards or self-talk, whatever your brain perceives, it believes.

Keeping Score With Self-Talk

An example of the power of self-talk came from Julie, a young high school junior who was taking my course. An avid golfer, Julie desperately wanted to earn a golf scholarship to college. "But I have to shoot an 85, and the lowest I've ever shot is a 92!" she lamented. "Will changing my self-talk help my golf score?"

We decided it couldn't hurt.

I asked Julie to walk around our circle of chairs, look each of us in the eye and say, "I'm shooting an 85 this summer." At first she resisted, but by the end of the circle we could hear a new determination in her voice. We applauded her for having the courage to say her dream out loud.

Later that week while out golfing with her father, Julie shot her first 85. A fluke? Perhaps. But if you argue with Julie, she'll ask you to explain how she won a tournament just two weeks later with an 80. She'll also ask you to explain why just about every pro golfer has a sports psychologist on their staff.

Julie got her golf scholarship and called to thank me. She added that there was one negative upshot, however.

"What's that?" I asked.

"Now my top competitor has caught onto self-talk!" she giggled.

We both knew that with life's wonderful abundance, Julie's mind-set was the only real hindrance, and she had now learned to get out of her own way.

After experiencing events like these, I don't have to give teens lectures on why the hopeless lyrics of many of today's songs are bad for them. They learn from life experience that what you put into your mind will come out in your life.

As a man thinks, so he is.
Proverbs 23:7

Using Affirmations

To help achieve our dreams and goals, it's not only important to avoid negative self-talk, but to replace it with positive affirmations. Since our computer brain is so responsive to whatever we tell it, why not program it for the very best? Affirmations are simply positive programming.

The most effective affirmations have four characteristics in common. They are:

- Personal (I)
- Present Tense (am)
- Pleasurable (enjoying)
- Positive (new characteristic)

When I add "positive" to the list, I am often asked how an affirmation could be anything but positive. I explain that the brain works on pictures and has no picture for the word "not." Therefore, the brain sees a picture of the negative behavior, and this can be counterproductive.

For example, for the phrase "I will not smoke anymore," there is no clear picture of not-smoking. We can replace this less effective phrase with a more vivid one, such as, "I am enjoying clean, clear lungs."

When writing an affirmation, it is important to be as specific as you can. The phrases, "I am enjoying weighing 135 pounds," and "I am enjoying making $50,000 a year," follow all of the above guidelines.

Finally, for the best results, say your affirmations three to five times a day. To help remind yourself, you could post a note in the middle of your mirror. Or you could use your car keys. As a reminder, every time you touch them, repeat the affirmations, telling yourself that the "key" to success is to change your mind.

------------------------ EXERCISE ------------------------

Take a moment to write two or three affirmations for yourself, using the above four steps. Avoid general futuristic phrases like, "I will be more peaceful and serene."

Remember, the brain cannot accomplish anything tomorrow. Rather, use a present tense verb, such as, "I am becoming more grateful and joyful with each passing day."

Here are some affirmations to get you started:

- I am intelligent, capable, loving, and lovable.
- I accept myself, unreservedly and completely.
- I set and accomplish my goals with ease.
- I make decisions quickly, easily, and confidently.
- I welcome good health and abundant wealth into my life at all times, and I use both in a loving manner.
- I am a loving parent/friend, who cares for others in tender and loving ways.
- I care for my body in a loving way and give it regular, fun exercise.
- I set and respect my own limits and boundaries in a considerate, yet assertive manner.
- I attract healthy, loving, and fulfilling relationships into my life and nurture them in a healthy manner.
- I have enough time, energy and resources to accomplish all that I desire.

- I have been given everything I need to live an abundantly happy, healthy life.

Many skills can be used to improve our attitude. None is easier or more immediately effective than changing what we say to ourselves.

All that we are arises with our thoughts.
With our thoughts we make the world.
Buddha

Habit D: Dream And Set Goals

Go confidently in the direction of your dreams.
Live the life you've imagined.
Henry David Thoreau

Years after the filming of the movie *Field of Dreams*, a line of cars still winds down the road in Dyersville, Iowa, to visit a little baseball field in the middle of nowhere. It was estimated that over 50,000 tourists visited this site in 1994 alone, making it the most popular tourist attraction in the state.

Don Lansing, the owner of the farm used as a setting for the film, does not charge for the visits. "You don't see any litter. Never one pop can. If somebody drops something, seven people reach to pick it up."

As a local reporter wrote, "Whatever they all come searching for, they inevitably find. That much is clear from their expressions as they leave."

Life offers us all a field of dreams, but often there is a price to pay. Dreamers from Edison to Ghandi, Annie Sullivan to Eleanor Roosevelt, Abe Lincoln to Martin Luther King, all had dreams for which they were ridiculed, yet they knew their dreams were sacred, and they held to them.

The story of *Pinnochio* reminds us of the importance of dreams. Like Gepetto, the puppeteer, we must first carve out our dreams, then put them aside on a shelf until it is time to act on them. When that experience comes, we must begin to say them out loud - even if only to the kitten on our windowsill. Finally, we must follow our dreams no matter what happens - even if it lands us on the bottom of the ocean in the belly of a whale.

Look at how often dreams are sung about in our most popular children's classics. From Walt Disney's *Cinderella*, we hear "A dream is a wish your heart makes...." In *The Wizard of Oz*, Dorothy sings "and the dreams that you dare to dream really do come true...." Pop singer Mariah Carey crooned, "Lord knows, dreams are hard to follow, but don't let anyone take them away..." in her 1994 hit song *Hero*. In literature, we don't need to look far to see what happens to a dream that dies, as in *Death of a Salesman* or *Dead Poets Society*.

A 1993 movie titled *Rudy* is based on the true story of a young man who yearned to play football for the University of Notre Dame. His desire was so intense that he overcame bad grades, small stature, lack of exceptional talent, lack of money, and lack of support from family members. Yet, because he followed his dream, Rudy accomplished a feat no Notre Dame player accomplished before or since.

The world stands aside to let anyone pass who knows where he is going.
David Starr Jordan

Finally, we can never forget Martin Luther King's *I Have A Dream* speech, still an extremely powerful message decades later. Whenever we talk of being inspired by someone, we are usually referring to being touched by his or her dream of a better world. In order to find greater happiness, we must all stay in touch with our dreams.

Dream-Beams

Dreams are unbounded, sacred expressions placed in our hearts to burn brightly enough to see us through our darkest days. They give our life purpose and meaning. We can think of our dreams as beams of sunlight. Goals are the leaves of our tree, catching the golden rays and transforming them into food to nourish the world. Dreams must precede goals or the goal will not be life-giving. Goals must follow dreams or the dreams will scorch our souls.

Those who lose dreaming are lost.
Australian Aborigine Proverb

Some time ago, I realized I had never met a kid on drugs who still had a dream. When speaking with a prominent juvenile court judge in our state, I asked him what he found amidst all the tragedies he dealt with that gave him the greatest hope. The first program that came to his mind was one that took fourth-graders to college campuses for a day. "It gives them a dream," he said. "What they often lose early in life is hope."

Dreams are an energy source, not just for children, but for adults as well. My dreams motivate me to get up each morning and give my all. As the dream of this book draws closer to reality, already my next dreams are forming. Without a dream, we are simply going through the motions of life. Dreams are life-giving, and therefore dreamers are full of life.

------------------------ EXERCISE ------------------------

When we're not sure what our dreams are, I suggest the "Lottery Winner" game:

1) **Congratulations! You just won the lottery! It's your first year as a lottery winner; whatever will you do?**
2) **Wow! What a great first year you've had since winning the lottery. But you're kind of tired of what you did last year, so what will you do this year?**
3) **Gee Whiz! I can tell by looking at you that you're really tired now. All that go-go-go for the last two years.... Now all you want to do is come home.**
4) **Well, you've had a nice long rest. You wake up one morning and realize you want to do something else with your life. What is it?**

What would you do if you could do anything at all? That's your dream.

--

Jim Carey, an actor known for his zany comedy films, realized the importance of dreams. In an interview with Barbara Walters, he shared that in 1987, during a three-month stretch without work, he wrote out a check to himself for $10 million, "for services rendered." He then dated the check "1995" and put it in his billfold.

It was in February of 1995 that Carey received a real check for $10 million for a film he had just completed. When he buried the dream check with his father one month later, the actor explained, "His dream was realized through me."

EXERCISE

Take five minutes to write down your dreams for the next three to five years. Dream in abundance. Imagine that you have unlimited time, resources, support, energy, health, and motivation. What would you like your life to look like? Imagine your home, your friends, your waistline, your garden, your neighbors, your bank account, your hobbies, your spirituality, your family, your freedom, your state of mind.

A fun follow-up for this exercise is to check your dream-list twice a year. Keep it in a special place. Then every New Year's day or birthday, get out your dream list and update it, celebrating those dreams you have accomplished.

When I invite adults to do the above dreaming exercise, there are many who balk and busy themselves so as not to have time to do it. I ask them to think of what they enjoy doing so much that they lose track of time. But often they feel as though writing their dreams down, even just for themselves, is too painful because it may set them up for disappointment.

At this point, I encourage them to begin setting goals: small puzzle pieces of the bigger dream picture that are more concrete and easily do-able.

Winners can tell you where they are going,
what they plan to do along the way,
and who will be sharing the adventure with them.
Denis Waitley

A study of Harvard alumni found that ten years after graduation:

- 83% of the graduates had no specific goals that they could name, either personally or professionally.
- 14% had specific goals but had never written them down.
- 3% had written goals.

In an income comparison, the third group with written goals (3%) was making ten times as much as the first group with no goals (83%).

Don't just THINK it, INK it.
Refrigerator magnet

Many of us self-sabotage our goals by making them too broad or too general. Take a moment to complete this next exercise:

------------------------ EXERCISE ------------------------

1) Write down six or seven life roles. Include roles such as spouse, parent, employee/employer, home owner, and "friend to myself."
2) Now for each role, brainstorm three possible goals. Make them specific, small, and measurable, such as, "I will walk for 15 minutes three times this week."
3) Choose only one or two from the entire list to work on for the next few weeks.

Note: You may want to use a reminder of a rubber band around your wrist until the goal is accomplished.

--

As she was learning to set goals, one woman wrote, "I will be more patient." Because we cannot measure our success for broad, non-specific goals like this one, they set us up not only for disappointment but also for self-rejection. Instead, it is better to make our goals measurable and bite size. As one successful CEO told me, "I'd rather under-promise and over-deliver." We can always surpass our smaller goals if we wish.

I asked the woman for specific times when she was impatient and discovered she wanted to be more patient with her kids in the morning. She then changed her goal to, "I will lay out the kids' clothes the night before school three times this week." It was a small enough goal which she could measure, achieve, celebrate, and adjust as needed.

Picking A Priority

A stumbling block I see in many frustrated goal-setters is that they do not maintain focus on their top priority. To say, "I really want to lose this weight" is wonderful. To then give in to the chips at every party you're invited to is torture. You must remind yourself every day of your top priority, and put everything else second, in order to overcome obstacles.

Whenever you watch a superior athlete, remind yourself of the parties and playtimes they turned down in order to be the best. When our eyes are focused on our goal, the sacrifices are not as painful. We must *pick* our priority and then *picture* our priority.

Visualization

The most successful people in any endeavor are those who practice the thoughts and feelings of success even before that success occurs. One of the most powerful techniques for this is visualization. Everyone who can think of what their home looks like without having to be standing in front of it can visualize. It's simply seeing with the mind's eye.

Visualization is a good friend of mind.
Anonymous

In her book, *The Joy of Visualization*, Valerie Wells says, "A picture is worth a thousand words, and visualizing is worth a thousand efforts." As far back as the nineteenth Century B.C., Virgil said, "Mind moves matter."

Arnold Schwarzennegger commissioned artists' drawings of his body at a more well-defined level than had ever been achieved by a body-builder. He knew he could achieve what he could conceive. Those were the pictures, according to Schwarzenegger, that helped him surpass all previous accomplishments in definition and muscle mass.

The best news, perhaps, is that this powerful mind-sight tool is easy. It takes just 5 - 10 minutes of your day or week. When you're sitting down, simply take a couple of deep breaths and daydream about how things will be when your goals are accomplished. Imagine not only the pictures of success, but the smells, tastes, and sounds as well. Visualize in 3-D! The clearer the image, the easier it will be for your incredible brain-computer to "get with the picture."

My wanting to be Mr. Universe came about
because I saw myself so clearly,
being up there
on the stage and winning.
Arnold Schwarzenegger

A Dream Deferred

Every so often we hear, "Dreamers have their heads in the clouds!" This is true. We must rise above the crowd, above the status quo, to dream. The key to success is to also keep our feet on the ground and our nose to the grindstone until we have found fulfillment.

I am reminded of my desire to make a TV commercial thanking my adopted daughter's birth mother, whom I had never met. The entire 30 second spot was planned out in my mind when I called five different organizations I thought might help me. They all thought it was a good idea. None of them, however, volunteered any support.

Four years later, I got a call from one of the gentlemen I had contacted. He said he had seen my commercial. Since I appeared frequently on camera, I asked which commercial he was referring to. "The one you called me about a few years back, the adoption commercial. It's powerful, Mary Kay, and it's touching women like you wouldn't believe." When I told him I had never followed through with the idea, he was truly amazed. What he had seen was someone else's effort that was exactly as I had described. While he affirmed me for my idea, I mourned not having the persistence and courage to complete the project years before.

Dreaming For Our Kids

A friend of mine had a dream for his inner-city grade school: that every child would have the opportunity to attend not only the finest high schools, but the finest colleges in the area.

Four years after he began to share this dream with others, he received funding from a prominent citizen in the community to offer every graduating eighth-grader both gifts. If the students stay out of trouble with the law, do not get pregnant, and achieve passing high school grades, their reward is a full four-year scholarship to one of seven colleges and universities in the area.

The grade school and its achievements have been honored dozens of times by educators and presidents. But its greatest reward is the track record for success these hope-full children have begun.

Look around you right now. Everything you see, including the furniture you're sitting on, began in someone's mind. So must our dreams.

Imagination sets the goal 'picture'
which our automatic mechanism works on.
We act, or fail to act, not because of 'will'
as is so commonly believed,
but because of imagination.
Maxwell Maltz

A young man from an inner-city high school once asked me if I wasn't feeling empty now that so many of my dreams had come true. I assured him that the joy I felt from having accomplished my past dreams only gave me courage to dream bigger dreams.

Then I asked him if there were still people hurting in the world. "Of course!" he said.

"As long as there are," I assured him, "I'll never run out of dreams. And neither will you."

Our corporation, INsight INc., has changed thousands of lives. In the early months of our business, I remember a phone call from one of my relatives. As I told him of my new venture, his response was, "Oh, everything you're into is such a fad!" I politely told him that my dream was too young and fragile to survive such harsh words, and I needed to end the phone call. He later apologized, recommended my tape series to a friend, and subscribed to our newsletter.

Sometimes, when we first give life to our dreams, we must protect them from attack. But following our dreams is always worth the effort. When we follow them, not only do we find happiness, but as Gepetto discovered, everyone around us becomes more real.

I am only one, but still I am one;
I cannot do everything,
but still I can do something;
and because I cannot do everything,
I will not refuse to do the something that I can do.
Edward Everett Hale

Habit E: Expect the Best

The real act of discovery consists not in finding new lands, but in seeing with new eyes.
Marcel Proust

"If you look the right way, you can see the whole world is a garden." After viewing the movie, *The Secret Garden*, this was the line that stayed with my 5-year-old. While the credits rolled, he turned to me and asked, "Mom, what's the *right* way?" I told him that was a wonderful question that would take me a lifetime to answer.

How we perceive life affects how much we enjoy life. Individuals with positive attitudes are optimistic; they expect the best. Although not everyone is raised with this mind-set, it can be learned. And once we understand the extraordinary benefits of optimistic thinking, we will want to do just that.

Optimism is a set of beliefs based on the following tenets:

1) The bad things in life are temporary (limited in time).
2) The bad things in life are small or insignificant (limited in scope).
3) I have control over my environment.

Pessimistic beliefs are based on the opposite tenets:

1) The good things in life are temporary.
2) The good things in life are small or insignificant.
3) I have little or no control. Rather, I am a victim of my environment.

It has been said, "Optimists and pessimists are both right about the same number of times. Optimists just enjoy life more." I believe even this quote is too pessimistic. I believe that optimists, because they help create the good they expect, are right 90% of the time, and do not waste time worrying about the other 10%.

One of my good friends was once confronted by a co-worker

with, "You aren't really happy. You just *think* you're happy!"

To which my friend replied, "Yeah, you're probably right, but my self-brainwashing is a wonderful way to live." How happy we are is all in our minds.

What are some of the advantages of thinking optimistically? Optimistic and hopeful thinking relaxes us. Relaxation results in increased blood flowing to the brain, which equals increased creativity and increased energy. In his wonderful book, *Learned Optimism*, Martin Seligman, Ph.D., cites hundreds of studies demonstrating that optimists:

- are healthier
- give up less easily
- are more successful in school and on the job
- are more successful on the playing field
- are more successful in relationships
- are depressed less often, for shorter periods of time

In short, if we want to be happy, optimism is our thinking pattern of choice.

Making optimism a way of life
can restore your faith in yourself.
Lucille Ball

In order to become more optimistic, we need to understand and assume the thoughts and behaviors of an optimistic individual. First, let's look at the three beliefs of optimists and pessimists in greater detail.

Temporary vs. Permanent

First, a pessimist believes negative events are permanent. An optimist believes negative events are temporary. One adversity, i.e. "I didn't get the job," is seen as a temporary setback for the optimist. "No problem. I've heard it takes three to six months of looking to secure a really good position."

From the same job rejection, the pessimist might conclude, "I'll never get a job." The pessimist sees one negative as just the beginning of bad things ahead and concludes, "I'm doomed."

------------------------ EXERCISE ------------------------

OPTIMISM QUIZ: This exercise will help you determine if you are generally optimistic or pessimistic. Take a moment to reflect on your life in recent years. Which have you interpreted as temporary flukes?

- **When things go well or poorly?**
- **People treating you well or badly?**
- **Good government or corrupt government?**
- **Peace or discord?**
- **Health or illness?**
- **Success or failure?**

If you answered that the positive options above were the temporary components of life, you tend toward pessimism. According to Seligman, pessimistic thinking can be reversed. "One of the most significant findings in psychology in the last twenty years is that individuals can choose the way they think." To think otherwise would, in itself, be pessimistic.

In the midst of winter, I finally learned that there was in me an invincible summer.

Albert Camus

Exaggeration Of The Negative

The second tendency of pessimists is to expand the areas effected by a negative event into "everyone," or "everything I do." The times I have listened to individuals immersed in despair, they often greatly exaggerate the scope of the painful events in their lives. One negative encounter, such as rudeness from a salesperson, becomes "(all) people are so rude anymore."

Take away their ability to exaggerate the negative, and we rob pessimists of their doom and gloom philosophy. Optimists, on the other hand, tend to restrict the negative influence to the specific occurrence or individual involved, while holding onto their personal power to take action and change it next time. An optimistic response the first time a salesperson is rude might be, "He was probably just having a bad day." If it happened again, an optimist might decide to call the manager and complain or change stores.

Action vs. Brooding

Finally, because of their belief in their own power, optimists tend to be action-oriented rather than ruminators, according to Seligman. Their rosier view of the world encourages action, and their actions create a rosier world. Pessimists tend to live more in their heads. They see other people and circumstances as having control over their lives and often fall into a "What's the use?" mentality. They feel helpless, which in turn makes them more hopeless.

"No Victims, only Volunteers" thinking and ownership of personal power create greater optimism.

We have been taught to believe that negative equals realistic and positive equals unrealistic.

Susan Jeffers
author of *Feel The Fear And Do It Anyway*

Better, Not Bitter

Optimists not only believe that the negative is limited in time and scope, they often see it as a blessing. They truly believe that good will come from pain. As an example, at a fairly early age, Martin Seligman had the misfortune to watch his father's debilitating helplessness from multiple strokes. Yet, it was only because of this painful circumstance that Seligman began his research into helplessness, giving hope to millions through his books and tapes on optimistic living.

These are not dark days; these are great days
- the greatest days our country has ever lived.
Winston Churchill

---------------------- EXERCISE ----------------------

Ask yourself these questions:

- **What is it you expect? Do you get it?**
- **Do you know people who almost always choose to expect the best?**
- **How do you react to their optimism? With envy, mockery, disbelief, or heightened motivation?**

The Optimist-Pessimist Game

To improve our awareness of how negative or positive our mind-set is at any given time, we can practice optimism in the form of a game.

The following stories are real life experiences. With a friend, see who can think up the worst, most exaggerated possible negative outcome for each occurrence. Then, see who can visualize the best, most exaggerated possible positive outcome for each one. After you've finished, turn the page to find out what really happened.

Example:

1) A 16 year-old's good friend fails to return her greeting as they pass in the hall between third and fourth period on a particular Monday morning.

Worst possible outcome thoughts: I know she's mad that I talked to Mark at the party Saturday....She'll never speak to me again!....I am a really fickle friend....I can't even study for Spanish, I'm too upset....Why can't I keep good friends?

Best possible outcome thoughts: She'll get over it....She'll understand when she finds out we were just talking about her....She's too good a friend to give up on us for one little thing....I can handle this....I'll talk to her after school and straighten things out....

Now it's your turn. Describe the worst and best possible outcomes for the following situations:

2) A young couple who has been trying to get pregnant for three years goes to a "Fertility of the Mind" seminar.
3) A banker is passed over for consideration for a promotion she thinks she honestly deserved.
4) Missing her keys, a teacher asks in the faculty lounge if anyone has seen them. She is told, "Kevin Smith probably took them. I'm glad you've got him this semester instead of me!"
5) A gentleman goes to the wrong airport in Washington D.C., and isn't able to make it to the correct one in time to catch his flight.
6) A teller at a branch office of a financial institution cashes a thousand dollar check for a customer, only to find that her computer was not updated in time to discover that the woman's account was closed.
7) A radio voice talent goes in for an audition, is told she is wonderful, and is then asked if she would be available the following Thursday. She tells the producer that Thursday would be great, but two Thursdays come and go with no call from the producer.
8) A 17-year-old doesn't find his name on the call-back list for the musical, even though he had the lead in the musical the year before.
9) A corporate trainer is doing a class on assertiveness when a young woman jumps up and runs out of the room.

How did you do? Was it easier to think optimistically or pessimisticaly? Compare your optimistic responses with the real-life outcomes that follow...

1) The 16-year-old girl's friend saw her after school and started chatting about things as usual. When the confused girl asked why she hadn't responded to the earlier greeting, her friend said she didn't even hear her, probably because she was worried about the chemistry test that was next on her schedule.
2) The couple came to the fertility seminar with a "What have we got to lose?" mentality. They sat in the front row, and the woman cried for most of the talk. The speaker encouraged them not only to remain hopeful, but to spend time around families with children and to envision themselves with their own brood. They had their first baby within the following year.
3) When the banker asked for a meeting with her boss to discuss why she wasn't recommended for the promotion, the shocked supervisor said she had no idea that the part-time employee wanted to start working full-time. The banker was promoted within the year.
4) Kevin Smith not only did not take the teacher's keys, he turned out to be one of the teacher's favorite students, ending the semester with a B+.
5) The gentleman decided to try and catch a flight from the "wrong" airport. The airline agents were able to get him on a plane leaving about the same time. The only seat left was in first class, which he was assigned with no extra charge.
6) The branch manager for the financial institution refused to give into discouragement, and prayed for the woman every day. Two weeks after taking the money, the woman came back into the bank and made full restitution.
7) The radio talent-wanna-be wrote a note to the producer after the second Thursday with no response, stating that she was going to call in two days to find out why she had not been contacted. "Whatever the reason, please just tell me the truth," the note read.

When she called, the producer was extremely apologetic. "We lost your phone number!" The woman started singing jingles the following week.

8) When the cast list was posted, the young man who was not called back discovered he had the lead part. The director explained that there was no reason to call him back. He was so strong, there was no competition for his role.
9) The woman returned to the class later, explaining that as she listened to the trainer, she realized she was rescuing her boyfriend. She had to call her mother immediately to change her instructions from, "Give him the $250 in the envelope," to, "Hide the envelope!"

Optimism is a fairly simple process of changing our thinking to expect the best and to realize our personal power. Yet, pessimism is still popular in modern society. Some people blame it on their childhoods saying, "It's how I was raised." Others are now claiming a genetic predisposition to pessimism. Notice the helplessness? It is pessimistic to believe that a negative event's effect has to last forever, or a gene can control your outlook on life.

Some people blame their pessimism on the media. It's true the media focuses on the negative. Yet why is the media so attentive to bad news? Because that's what we buy and watch. Study after study has shown that newspapers featuring negative headlines sell up to 10 times as many copies as positive ones.

Once, while visiting my parents in Fort Myers, Florida, the evening News-Press headline read, "Pessimism Kills Heart Patients." The newspaper could have bannered, "Optimism Saves Lives" but it would have sold fewer copies.

Perhaps we fill our heads with potential catastrophes to ensure that we are prepared for all the bad things that might happen. One attraction is that expecting the worst protects us from disappointment. However, our expectations often become self-fulfilling prophecies. The good news is we can teach ourselves to expect the best.

To learn to think more optimistically, here are the steps I call **The 4 A's of Affirmative Living.**

1) **Awareness** is being alert to a specific painful experience occurring right now in my life, and what my beliefs are about it.

2) **Acceptance** is owning that I have control over my beliefs and over my behaviors concerning the situation.

3) **Accurate Assessment** is substituting any pessimistic thinking with optimistic thinking. These optimistic beliefs might include:
   - people are basically good;
   - what goes around comes around;
   - we are never given a dream without the power to make it come true;
   - God works all things for good;
   - evolution is bringing the universe to greater order each moment;
   - I am right where I need to be today, this moment.

4) **Action** is following through on any behavior that results from the optimistic beliefs. This could include things like applying for the job, entering a contest, or asking for what we want from an individual or institution.

An example of how to use these four steps involved John, a man in his 30s, who was in a shelter where I was speaking one December. John began the class complaining about being extremely chilled at night with only one blanket on his bed. Despite the fact that he was not sleeping well as a result of being so cold, he was unwilling to ask for an additional blanket. His **4 A's** looked like this:

1) **Awareness** = Cold with only one blanket.
   The group helped John narrow the scope of the problem to a manageable size. It wasn't "the world" or

"this place" that was the problem. It was the lack of an additional blanket causing lack of sleep. He also become aware that, as a result, his work was suffering. His sleepiness impaired his concentration, and he was in danger of losing the job he so badly needed.

2) **Acceptance** = I can change the situation by taking action. John admitted that not doing anything wasn't helping. Therefore, he somewhat hesitantly owned that the person who needed to do some changing was himself.

3) **Accurate Assessment** = Correcting my pessimistic beliefs.
His belief was, "They kick you out for askin' for stuff like that!" When I asked where he got his information, he said someone at the last shelter he was in made it clear that such requests were taboo. Our class disputed John's thinking with evidence that this shelter's staff did not evict people for asking for what they needed in a courteous manner.

4) **Action** = Asking for what I want.
Using the skills discussed in Habit A, John asked to speak to the night clerk, who responded, "How many blankets do you want?" John's entire thinking pattern was changed by the event, and he was able to graduate from the shelter program and finish his college education within two years.

The world is as we are.
Old Ayurvedic Saying

How To Stay Optimistic

In order to stay optimistic, I follow these basic patterns:

1) I monitor my self-talk.

2) I strengthen my "hope-muscle" each week by reading stories of overcomers, both past and present, who beat the odds. Books such as *Chicken Soup for the Soul*, by Jack Canfield and Mark Victor Hansen, are excellent nourishment for a pessimistic mood.
3) I insulate myself from the barrage of negatives available each day in the media or in "downer" groups at work or at home.
4) I take risks and ask for what I want. I simply dare life to give me the best when I am feeling pessimistic. I might go to a party even though I'm afraid it will be dull and then be delightfully surprised. Life itself helps me become optimistic once again.

We don't always get what we deserve, but we almost always get what we expect. It's time we each decide to move from straining our brain with fear to training our brain to expect the best. We can choose to use the power of positive, self-fulfilling prophecies to forecast a future full of promise.

Everything that is done in the world is done by hope.
Martin Luther

Habit F: Feeling All Your Feelings

The young man who has not wept is a savage,
and the old man who will not laugh is a fool.
George Santayana

How important are feelings? They are the primary reason we have a job, or marry, or read a book. Ultimately, our goal in life is to feel good - joy - and to help others feel good. Life is all about feelings.

Yet sometimes, in an effort to feel good, we spend our entire lives running from feeling bad. What we need to remember is that we cannot experience the good feelings without allowing ourselves to feel the painful emotions. The suppression of one feeling tends to decrease feelings in general.

Think about a relationship. The only way you can guarantee you will not be hurt is to not care about the other person. As soon as you care, if the person moves to another city, you will feel the pain of sadness and loneliness. Similarly, if you never feel anger when a friend is being belittled, then you have already cut yourself off from caring about him or her. Feelings are all intertwined.

When I asked a successful children's therapist what he believed was the most important message for me to share with kids, he said, "Tell them to feel all their feelings." The natural response to such a mission is, "Why would we need to teach them to feel? Isn't feeling something children do naturally?"

The answer is yes, children do feel their feelings naturally...until they are taught to do otherwise. Unfortunately, as we were growing up, many of us were taught to shut off from our emotions. When we were hurting or upset, we were told to "forget it," "don't worry about it," or that we "shouldn't feel that way." Even when I speak to children today, I continue to hear that they have been taught a fear and distrust of feelings.

The Feelings Class

In a short talk to a class of second-graders, I asked them a question that had no correct answer. "Would you help me list the good and bad feelings?" Knowing that feelings are neither good nor bad, I simply wanted to hear their perceptions.

Not surprisingly, they had no trouble naming the feelings they were "not supposed to feel." The two emotions they all agreed to put into this negative category were "sad" and "mad."

I then told the children a "what if" story.

> Let's imagine I'm a fairy godmother who can make these 'bad' feelings go away. All you have to do is ask me. But before you decide to do that, let's imagine one more thing. Let's say I take your anger away, and tomorrow is show and tell day. You've decided to take your new puppy to school.
>
> Recess is right before show and tell, so you take your puppy out onto the playground. Suddenly, the fourth-grade bully walks up and starts teasing you as he pulls the puppy's tail. Then he grabs the puppy right out of your hands and throws it up into the air. The puppy is crying because it's so scared. What are you going to do?

"Stop him!" "Go get help!" "Tell him to stop!" I hear from the kids.

"But wait, you aren't even angry, remember? I took away all your anger the day before, so this wouldn't even bother you, right?"

After a moment of stunned silence, I ask if anyone wants to keep his or her anger. They all do. "And who do we need to protect with our anger energy every day?" I ask.

"Me."

Anger is energy for protection or energy for change. I call it "Angergy." The kids catch on quickly. With adults it sometimes takes longer.

Action is the antidote to despair.
Joan Baez

I learned a lot about anger energy when I was in counseling right after my divorce. "Mary Kay, why are you smiling while you describe all these painful events?" my counselor asked during one of my sessions.

"Am I smiling? It must be because I've forgiven him."

"No," she said calmly. "You can't forgive something until you've faced it, and you are just beginning to face what has happened. Go home and write down every abusive incident from the past six years."

Eleven single-spaced pages later, I was no longer smiling. I got in touch with my repressed anger and was amazed at its power. I had so much energy that I walked for at least an hour a day. I've never been in such great physical shape as during that year of working out my anger.

The best patients are very open about their anxiety, hostility, their emotions in general.... Whenever a nurse tells me a patient is a nuisance who keeps questioning everything, I respond, "Good, he's going to live longer."
Dr. Bernie Siegel, M.D.
from his video: *Hope and a Prayer*

Depression And Rage

The clinical definition of depression is anger turned inward. It is obvious that depression results in a lack of energy, while rage is the release of pent-up energy. When we repress our anger, we have no energy, or explode inappropriately.

One of the main reasons women become depressed more often than men is that women are often unwittingly taught that if they get in touch with their anger, they'll have to wear a black, pointed hat for the rest of their lives. The good news is more and more women are now realizing that anger is a healthy emotion everyone needs to feel and release.

"But it might turn into rage!" I hear from both men and women. I simply share that after my first marriage, my ex-husband's program for recovery was similar to mine: to get in touch with his anger. Learning to feel and express anger prevents rage. How? By dealing with upsetting events one at a time.

A Ton Of Bricks

Think of an anger-event as a brick. When an upsetting situation occurs, it is often caused by someone "crossing our boundaries." Our feelings of anger tell us to set the boundary more clearly next time.

Now suppose the person we need to communicate with is our supervisor, and we have the distinct impression that even the gentlest communication of our boundary will result in the loss of our job. The result might be that our brick of anger, rather than being shared at the time, is stored in our rage bag.

Ragers tend to hold things in and then throw their emotional bag of bricks onto another person's head over fairly minor issues. Had the rager dealt with each upset individually, or asked for what he or she wanted and set limits as needed, the rage would not have occurred.

------------------------ EXERCISE ------------------------

The next time an event upsets you, get out a piece of paper and answer this question:

"How does it feel?" or "How do I feel?"

Then keep answering the following question over and over:

"How else does it feel?" or "How else do I feel?"

Keep writing until you feel a shift in how you feel or a release of energy.

--

Am I My Feelings?

We are not our feelings. As author Anthony De Mello, S.J., wrote in his book *Awareness*, "We are the sky. Our feelings are in the clouds." Therefore, I discourage the use of phrases such as, "I *am* angry right now." The more accurate phrase would be, "I *feel* pretty angry right now."

Our brain listens to how we phrase such descriptions of our mental well-being. Feelings of anger or frustration are temporary signals that an imbalance has occurred. Acknowledging them simply helps us get back in balance. Granted, there are days we feel "overcast," but we can only deal with one cloud at a time.

A Cry For Help

The other most suppressed feeling is sadness, which in the past, men tended to suppress more often than women. "Wimp!" and "Cry-Baby!" are just two of the labels society uses to belittle those who allow themselves to cry. Yet crying is our primary mechanism for releasing tension.

Mad and sad are two sides of the same emotional coin. Every event that we feel angry about, we also feel some sadness over, and vice-versa. The goal is to feel both sides of the coin. Then our sads or mads won't overwhelm us.

**If a person can say, 'I don't feel anything,'
then he has cut off from feeling his own aliveness.
This statement is heard from
those who are clinically depressed.**

Alexander Lowen, M.D.
author of *The Spirituality of the Body*

We cry not only when we feel desperate, but when our desperation lifts. A mother who cannot locate her child does not cry while she is frantically searching for him, but only after she has found him.

A dear friend of mine shared with me that she wept deeply the first time she and her husband made love. She had connected with the child inside her and with a lost feeling of pure joy.

When my son was three, he would often ask why I was crying during times of joy. I said I was letting go of my "happy tears." One day while watching a happy ending of a movie with me, he became very excited. "Look, Mom!" he exclaimed as he pointed to his cheeks. "I have happy tears now, too!"

------------------------ EXERCISE ------------------------

Ask yourself:

"If someone referred to me as 'emotional,' how would I choose to respond?"

"When am I uncomfortable sharing my feelings or having others share their feelings with me?"

I recently heard someone remark, "People are emotionally constipated!" I chuckled, but I had to agree. One reason we are so emotionally repressed could be the result of the painful experiences of our great or great-great grandparents.

In the early days of this nation, all families lost children to death on a regular basis. Their allotted time for grieving was sometimes half an hour before the wagon train moved on, or before the plantation master returned home. Family members had to suppress their emotions to survive.

Whatever reasons people used to have for shutting down emotionally, they no longer exist. It's time we allowed ourselves to *feel* better.

The Man Who Dared Not Cry

After my divorce, I participated in a weekend retreat called "Beginning Experience"with other divorced and widowed singles. While the other six members of my small group and I cried freely, one very solidly built farmer in his early 30s remained silent and did not shed a tear - until the last day.

We were invited to write good-bye letters to our former spouses to gently close the door on our past. Then, anyone who wanted to read his or her letter was invited to do so. One by one, in a powerful sharing, everyone in the group read their letters except the young farmer. Courageously, the facilitator asked if he too would like to read the letter he held in his hand.

I then witnessed something that left a great impression on me. This huge man, whose body was as rigid as a cement block, began to crumble. At first, he just choked, as the frightened part of him struggled to hold back the emotions that another part of him was straining to release. Two group members ran to hold him as he shook violently. Finally, his huge chest, perhaps so large because it had held so much for so long, began to heave in convulsing sobs.

As he wept violently, he told us he worked on a farm with his father. He shared that his two-year-old daughter had died three years before, and that his father's response to any mention of his little girl's name had always been to look down at the ground.

"I started to do the same thing whenever my wife would talk about her. It's no wonder she left me. I shut down my heart to any feelings," he poured out to us. He then read us a good-bye letter, not to his wife - he said that would come later - but to his little girl.

I have always felt sorry for people afraid of feeling,
of sentimentality,
who are unable to weep with their whole heart.
Golda Meir

No Tears Allowed

Anyone who watched the '96 Olympics in Atlanta might recall a painful scene. 19-year-old Shannon Miller, with one small mistake, slipped from medal contention to a distant tenth place in the women's individual gymnastics standings. TV viewers listened in as the coach of this extremely young team exhorted her to stop crying. "Suck it up!" he exclaimed to the young woman whose dreams had just come crashing down. His words were one more indictment against the "sin" of crying.

"How are you feeling?" we ask someone who is recovering from an illness. It is time we ask *ourselves* how we are feeling our feelings. At this point in history, the only thing that is keeping us from experiencing all of our feelings is our fear of them. It's time we allow our children and ourselves to answer, "I'm feeling (my feelings) really well."

Getting into the Flow

One of the most amazingly simple techniques to help us feel our feelings is to breathe deeply. Dr. Lowen says "to breathe deeply is to feel deeply."

Often we busy ourselves to the point that we remark we "barely have time to breathe." When Lowen had patients who were suppressing a feeling, they were usually holding their breath. The simple instruction to breathe helped release their emotions.

Body-Mind author Louise Hay suggests a similar technique when dealing with fear: "When you get scared, become aware of your breath as it flows in and out of your body. Recognize that your breath, this most precious substance, is freely given to you. You have enough to last for as long as you live. Take a deep breath, go within, and understand that life will support you in whatever way you need it to."

Other techniques I find helpful for feeling mad or sad:

- Check my comments for sarcasm (anger that isn't getting validated).
- Check for a lump in my throat or for a scratchy throat.
- Beat a pillow, stamp my feet, or throw eggs at trees.
- Journal anything and everything that comes to mind.
- Take a walk and express aloud to myself or to my walking partner the feelings that come to me. I do not analyze, judge, or try to "fix" my feelings. I simply give them a voice.
- Rent a sad movie (*An Affair to Remember* or *My Life*).
- Start or join a support group such as the 12-step Emotions Anonymous.
- Seek out a good counselor.

EXERCISE

Here is an interesting game for all ages:

1) **Write 20 different feelings on slips of paper.**
2) **Put the 20 slips in an envelope.**
3) **One person pulls out a feeling word and reads it aloud.**
4) **Everyone in the group shares a time when he or she felt that feeling.**
5) **When all have shared, someone else pulls out another slip of paper, and the game continues.**

This game can lead to discussions of what we do when we feel certain feelings, how what we think affects what we feel, as well as how all feelings are temporary.

Feeling As Sensing

Every emotion is a feeling, but not every feeling is an emotion. Some feelings are more like sensations. Intuition is a kind of sensing feeling that everyone possesses to some degree. Once discovered, it can greatly enrich our lives.

The founder of Sony was asked by best-selling author Deepak Chopra how he became so financially successful without ever taking any business courses. Chopra was told, "I swallow the deal. If it gives me indigestion, I don't do it."

There are three signs of intuition. The first is that my thought is not rational. It does not make logical sense. Secondly, it will repeat itself. The irrational thought will return after I've dismissed it as "silly." Finally, true intuition is always rooted in love and would never encourage hurtful behaviors.

EXERCISE

Feelings are not simply a mental process; they involve the body. Here are two exercises I learned from Cathryn Taylor, author of *The Inner Child Workbook*:

Pre-step: Relax your body by taking two deep breaths, holding each breath for a few seconds, and then exhaling. Once your body is relaxed, visualize one of your parents. With your eyes closed, ask yourself where you "carry" this parent. For example, I "feel" my father in my throat area, or I "feel" my mother in my heart area. Each person is unique in this respect.

Next: Take a moment to think back to a time when you felt embarrassed. Where do you feel this feeling?

Finally: Notice this week where you feel various feelings. Some people feel rejection in their "gut," while others feel it as a "stab in the back." You will discover that you tend to feel similar feelings in the same area of your body.

When we "go with the flow" of our feelings, we experience a sense of relief, non-judgement, connectedness with life, understanding of ourselves and others, and greater self-love. We cannot be free until we are free to feel.

To feel is to heal.

Eddy Buchanan
author of *Heartway to Heaven*

Habit G: Gratitude

If we learn how to give of ourselves,
forgive others,
and live with Thanksgiving,
we need not seek happiness.
It will seek us.
Anonymous

Beauty, babies, and other blessings....It's energizing and healing to focus on what we are grateful for. Often, this awareness comes only after loss. We lose a child, a sibling, a parent, or a friend and are much more appreciative of our living loved ones. We can learn about the importance of gratitude from wisdom or from woe. Wisdom is the easier path.

One of my "Gratitude Attitude" teachers was a man named Jim. One afternoon he shared this story with me:

> When I was in the war, survival and sanity were daily battles. One night as I was trying to sleep, I became greatly disturbed by the fact that my socks were wet. Amid the awfulness, this discomfort began to gnaw at me. I remember going to sleep that night promising God that if I could ever again go to sleep with dry socks on, I would be forever grateful.

When Jim survived the war, he kept his promise in the form of a daily gratitude list. Each night before retiring, he wrote out those things he was grateful for. At the age of 57, Jim was a happily married business owner of a thriving company. Then calamity struck. His major supplier went bankrupt. Jim lost the business as well as the beautiful home in the country that had been his wife's dream all their married life.

"Often times, the only thing on my gratitude list was 'dry socks,' but it got me through those hard times," Jim shared.

He who receives a benefit with gratitude, repays the first installment on his debt.

Seneca

One Of The Happiest People

When I had the opportunity to interview author Nathaniel Branden in 1993, I saw a picture of his wife on his desk and commented on her beauty. His face lit up as he described her as "one of the most consistently happy people I have ever known." In explaining what set her apart, Branden noted, "She almost never goes to sleep at night without taking time to review everything good in her life; these are typically her last thoughts of the day."

Gratitude costs nothing, but can yield great rewards. In our homes, gratitude is a small seed that can become a mighty oak. Many parents in my seminars complain that their children are ungrateful. I ask, "When do your children see parents who are grateful?"

One grandmother's comment after a lavish Thanksgiving meal at her son's home was, "Since we didn't say grace before dinner, could we please say 'thank you' afterwards?" Later she expressed sadness that this national holiday instituted to give thanks had become nothing more than an excuse to over-indulge in the abundance we've been given.

The Gratitude Attitude

A year after his heart attack, a gentleman in his 60s was asked by our local paper to describe the greatest change in his life during that twelve months. Without hesitation he said, "My attitude." The reporter asked for an example of what that change looked like.

"Now I have the gratitude attitude," the man replied. "Like, just this morning I was out jogging, saw some friends sitting on the porch, waved at them, and said, 'Great day to be above ground, isn't it?'"

Gratitude In The Workplace

What would our lives be like if we made a commitment to gratitude? On a professional level, gratitude could make a more significant positive impact than the introduction of computers. At a major corporation, one of my classes decided to look at the results of a recent "greatest needs" survey. The need for recognition topped the employees' needs list at the plant.

As the group discussed what could be done to address the problem, the first thoughts were to chastise those supervisors who were not recognizing the achievements of their team members. Slowly, it dawned on the class that they were doing the very thing they were condemning: finding fault rather than recognizing recognition. Thus, they came up with creative ways to recognize individuals in the plant.

The first person they decided to recognize was their CEO, a man they greatly admired as an individual and a leader. They discussed which method to use, and the idea of a green philodendrum plant symbolizing the "growing plant" won approval. "But what if he gets dozens of plants as gifts?" one gentleman asked. He then volunteered to contact the executive's secretary to see if that was the case.

What was reported back stunned the group. "Not only has he never received a plant or *any* gift from anyone here at the site these past five years, but when I went to see his secretary, she pulled out the only thank-you note she'd ever received. It was sent to her three years ago, and she's kept it all this time," the team member reported. "The people at the top don't get the recognition they deserve either."

The group also made a video of "Moments of Great Recognition" to share with the CEO and training department. One woman, who had been at the plant for over 25 years, shared that one of her happiest memories was the day her supervisor brought sugar-free cookies to a party because she knew this woman was diabetic - a small but significant gesture.

Blessed are those who can give without remembering, and take without forgetting.
Princess Bibesco

The Three Steps For Showing Appreciation

Remember the steps for asking for what you want covered in Habit A: "When you," "I feel," "Because?" The first three of the steps are a beautiful way to show gratitude as well.

Recently, I worked on this skill with a group of surgical technicians from area hospitals. After I taught the process, I asked for a volunteer to take the risk of using the first three of the four steps to thank someone present that day at the seminar.

A woman stood and said,

1) "Marilyn, when you encouraged me just now at break to consider a nursing career,
2) I felt really good, and very grateful,
3) Because it means you've been noticing my extra efforts. I just wanted you to know how much I appreciated your comments."

It stands out in my memory as the most powerful moment of the entire seminar.

Silent gratitude isn't much use to anyone.
Gladys Borwyn Stern

Expressing gratitude is a simple but powerful skill. As with all other risks, it takes courage. At one seminar I asked the audience members, "What is a risk you would like to take here at work, but haven't yet?"

One woman answered, "I would like to let people know how grateful I am to work here."

Gratitude is the attitude of the winners in life. "Of course," say the more cynical individuals. "I'd be grateful if I were a big winner, too." However, the winner's gratitude almost always came *before* they won.

The Grateful Greats

I was attending the awards banquet for a large real estate company as their keynote speaker. The awards preceding my talk were full of names I didn't recognize and numbers I didn't understand. But one number I could follow. Total sales for the year got higher as the plaques got larger.

The numbers went up incrementally until the final award. It took the emcee five minutes to list all of the achievements of a man named Paul. What was even more amazing was that Paul's sales total was nearly double that of the second place finisher. I fully expected a silver-haired, well-seasoned veteran to step forward amid the thunderous applause. Instead, a young man in his thirties with bright eyes and a sweet smile walked up to receive the award.

At the podium he thanked God, his family, his mentors, and his cohorts, as many do on such occasions. I made a mental note to talk with him after the banquet, but it was unnecessary. He was one of the first to seek me out.

"Thank you so much!" he said grabbing my hand. "I have believed and tried to live what you spoke about all my life. I am so grateful for your powerful words." He was obviously a man comfortable with expressing gratitude.

That same year, the winner of the U.S. Open golf tournament was Steve Jones, a man who had not won a tournament in over six years due to a hand injury from a biking accident. It was obvious to the announcers, as well as to the television audience, that during the last nine holes, the pros everyone expected to win were self-destructing through nerves.

After his startling victory, Steve was asked how he accomplished such a feat. Steve began the interview with, "First, I want to thank my Lord and Saviour, Jesus Christ". He went on to share with the interviewer that he just kept reminding himself how *grateful* he was to be playing in the finals of such a prestigious tournament, and that had kept his nervousness from winning out.

His first words were the same as those spoken just a few months earlier by Nebraska quarterback Tommie Frazier the day he won MVP for his second collegiate national championship in a row. It seems the greatest among us tend to be the most grateful.

Gratitude Among Friends

My women's group met recently. We hadn't seen each other in four weeks, and there was much catching up to do. Each person who shared had faced a major challenge during our time apart, and the tears flowed. When it was time to end our sharing, there was silence, until one woman said what was in all of our hearts. "I've never had friends like this before." Our tears became tears of gratitude.

Gratitude opens the heart and bridges the gaps. It is an antidote to despair and discouragement. It is not only freeing, it is free. We need pass no new laws or buy new books for our schools. We must simply be open to feeling it and committed to sharing it.

Blessings

Count your garden by the flowers,
Never by the leaves that fall;
Count your days by golden hours,
Don't remember clouds at all!
Count your night by stars, not shadows;
Count your life by smiles, not tears,
And on this and each tomorrow,
Count your age by friends, not years.

Laura Mae Utley Gibson

Habit H: Hugs And Touch

**RX for indigestion, insomnia, isolation, or the blues:
One fluffy puppy - to be snuggled at meals, at bedtime,
or when just home from a tough day at the office.**

When life is rubbing us the wrong way, touch can get us back *in touch* with our healthier and happier selves. It can relax and reassure us. In addition, this basic need *touches* us at a very primal level. The connection between human contact and well-being is far more than *skin deep*.

The Benefits Of Touch

Recent studies show a variety of benefits from touching:

- The arteries of rabbits fed a high-cholesterol diet and petted regularly had 60% less blockage than did the arteries of unpetted but similarly fed rabbits.
- Rats handled for 15 minutes a day during the first three weeks of their lives showed dramatically less memory loss as they grew old, compared with non-handled rats.
- Children and adolescents hospitalized for psychiatric problems demonstrated remarkable reductions in anxiety levels, as well as positive changes in attitude, when they receive a brief daily back rub.
- Patients in nursing homes fared better when regularly hugged by their family or friends.
- In countries where mothers work all day in the fields and carry their infants in slings, the children grow up more disease-resistant and better emotionally adjusted than those touched less.
- Adults who received regular massages had reduced tension and anxiety, increased circulation, and more of the feel-good brain chemicals called "endorphins."

Affection Affects Us

Touch heals - both individuals and relationships. In connecting us with others, touch reconnects us with an inner healing potential that is not otherwise activated. Research is beginning to bring us a clearer understanding of how healing energy is heightened through touch. For now, let's consider what happens when a four-year-old scrapes his knee.

"I fell down!" Mom hears between sobs. What the child is doing is instinctive: placing his hand over the wound, and running to Mom to have her kiss it or touch it. Studies now indicate that Mom's hand often becomes warm to hot as she caresses the wound. "The warmth of a Mother's love," is more than just a figure of speech, as is "the heat of passion."

So how do we incorporate back into our lives the natural healing behavior of touch? We can either reconnect with our bodies, or we can first learn to be emotionally sensitive. Our bodies will then follow suit. To be loved, we must be love-able; that is, able to love. We must learn to open our hearts and be vulnerable, emotionally as well as physically.

Any rigidity of my body prevents me from vibrating in resonance with others.

Alexander Lowen, M.D.
author of *Spirituality of the Body*

Think of a very muscular individual with his or her arms crossed over their chest. Does this stance invite a hug? Hardly. The message is, "I do not need anyone. Stay away." A board and an iron bar cannot hug because they are too stiff. So, quite often, it is our emotional stiffness that holds us back from reaching out to others through touch. Take this quick inventory to see how emotionally flexible or rigid you tend to be:

EXERCISE

- **How stubborn would your friends say you tend to be?**
- **Can you back down when you're wrong and apologize?**
- **When you feel the need, can you back up and start over?**
- **Can you change your mind/direction without undue embarrassment?**
- **Do you often empathize to the point of feeling *with* someone rather than sorry *for* them?**
- **How spontaneous are you when someone proposes an outing?**
- **Check areas of your life such as family, friends, and work to see if you tend to get into ruts, or if you are a person who constantly sees new possibilities with enthusiasm.**

When we care about others, as healthy individuals do, we allow ourselves to show vulnerability both emotionally and physically. Rigid bodies and hardened hearts cause physical and emotional illness.

The Anti-Touch Taboos

Why don't more of us "keep in touch?" The amount of contact we are comfortable with may partially depend on our geographic roots. One study in the '60s noted the number of touches exchanged by people sitting in coffee shops around the world:

- In Puerto Rico, people touched each other 180 times per hour.
- In Paris, France, 110 times per hour.
- In Gainesville, Florida, two times per hour.
- In London, England, according to the study, the researchers are still waiting for someone to touch their companion at a coffee shop!

Challenges And Choices

There are many factors that have fueled the anti-touch sentiment that seems to pervade our schools and our workplaces. Some of the most powerful barriers are as follows:

1) CHALLENGE: Many child-rearing professionals in the past few decades have either implied or stated outright that a baby can be spoiled by too much holding. This resulted in infants spending hours in their cribs.
RESPONSE: We now know that the more a baby is touched, held, and breast-fed, the healthier the baby will be, both physically and emotionally. (A 1996 study indicated that breast-feeding may help reduce SIDS deaths, along with placing the baby on his/her back when sleeping.)

2) CHALLENGE: The first days in the lives of present day adults were often spent in a crib of a hospital ward rather than in their parents' arms. This trend began with babies born in the '40s. It worsened in the '50s, when mothers were only encouraged to have occasional visits with their newborns so they could rest. This resulted in emotional wounding rather than the bonding so important to an infant's development.
RESPONSE: We need to reaffirm, in every way, a parent's and baby's need to touch each other in the first moments, days, months, and years of the baby's life. This includes having the infant with the parent(s) at all times in the hospital unless there is a special circumstance creating a need for separation.

   One of my greatest sadnesses in life is that I did not fight to be with my newborn adopted daughter. My employer did not allow me the six weeks of parental leave commonly offered because I was adopting rather than delivering. I was in an emotional upheaval and did not take a stand. Consequently, my baby and I both paid a dear price.

3) CHALLENGE: Ten years ago, I heard a grandfather say to his five-year-old grandson who had just climbed excitedly onto his lap, "We don't do this anymore. You're five now." The fear of being labeled as "gay" has frightened many men and women into denying and suppressing their need for touch.
RESPONSE: In Poland and Italy, adult women friends of all ages and sexual preferences walk the streets hand in hand and arm in arm. We must let go of "what people will think" long enough to ask what it is we want and need. Then we must trust that our inner wisdom will lead us to healthier habits of touch.

4) CHALLENGE: The sexual harassment cases that have received so much media attention often fail to address the lack of assertiveness of the victims. Part of the problem is that women have silently put up with inappropriate behavior for too long. We need to own our responsibility in this regard.
RESPONSE: Rather than blaming others for past patterns, we can take responsibility with a phrase such as: "I helped train individuals to continue the behavior with my silence. That was then. This is now. Today I shall choose to set limits and stand by them."

5) CHALLENGE: Sexual misconduct with children is the most serious and dangerous touch issue. Since fewer families live in close-knit neighborhoods and small towns, we often find ourselves leaving our children at day-cares, birthday parties, or scout meetings with virtual strangers.
RESPONSE: Involvement with our children's friends, personal screening and strict precautions are necessary. A good friend of mine put together a social "Lock-in" for the moms of her grade school in order to get to know them better. They knew it was a huge success when the parking lots jammed for the rest of the school year with mothers exchanging greetings and information.

> I once hired a cleaning lady who was bonded and insured, but we later discovered that she was also wanted for theft by the U.S. Marshal. I now screen everyone who comes into my home for weeks before hiring them.

Teachers And Touching

Can we err on the side of too much caution? I believe so. For example, once instructors are screened and deemed appropriate and fit to teach our children, we must allow them to touch those they teach. Fear of being sued is sometimes translated by wary school administrators as, "Hands off." If the purpose of schools is learning, we must face the fact that students learn better from teachers who touch them.

An excellent example of the touching-teaching link was shared with me by a therapist. His friend, also a therapist, had been working with a woman for six months with little success. Considering ending their sessions, he was thrilled when, at the following appointment, the woman described accomplishing the goals they had set for her.

"What happened to finally motivate you to do all this?" the therapist asked.

"I just did what my hair stylist suggested."

Fascinated, the therapist began to study how touch helps relax people and open them up. The results of his study were so astounding, he changed his career course. Today he teaches therapy techniques to hair stylists all across the country.

A powerful example of our need to touch our children is in *Chicken Soup for the Soul*, Volume I. The story is simply called, "The Hand." It's about a kindergartner who is asked to draw something he is grateful for at Thanksgiving time. No one in the class, including the teacher, guesses what his simple drawing of a hand represents. It turns out, he is most grateful for the teacher who allows him to put his hand in hers at recess.

If we want to touch our children's lives, we must touch our children. Imagine a law in our schools forbidding eye contact with students. (After all, a lascivious wink from a teacher to a student could harm that child for life!) We must come back to our senses - all of them.

Touching Through Hugs

One "touching" technique accessible to us all is the human hug. I'll never forget the day my former mother-in-law asked me to teach her how to hug. Her son and I had just returned from a short vacation, and I was hugging her daughter. When I greeted the older woman with a smile and a "Hello," she asked, "Why don't I ever get a hug?"

Stunned, I assured her it was not an intentional slight; I just wasn't aware that she was comfortable hugging. "I would be if someone would show me how." From that time on, we hugged. It was as simple as that.

The Happy Hugger

A similar incident was responsible for winning my Dad over to hugging. Tom, a boy I dated in college, was known on campus as "The Happy Hugger." Whether with men, women, professors, or janitorial staff, he spread love through hugs wherever he went.

The first time I brought Tom home to meet my parents, I failed to warn him that my "Dr." Dad was not of the hugging persuasion. So when we walked into my home together, Tom swept Dad off his feet with a huge bear-hug. My family and I stood there, stunned and silent, as Dad, just as surprised, collected himself.

Four days later, when it was time for us to return to campus, Tom extended his hand to Dad, and he was swept off his feet by hugging's newest devotee.

The Hugging Manager?

I'll always remember giving my first training course for managers. It was one of my most challenging assignments. Throughout the course, three gentlemen maintained very tight and closed body language. Their arms crossed over their chests spoke to me of protecting themselves, especially their hearts, from being touched.

I planned a special graduation ceremony for the final day of class and brought three professional massage therapists and their massage chairs with me. I tucked them all into adjoining rooms and proceeded into the classroom. After congratulating the participants on their hard work, I passed out a journaling exercise. "I want you to collect your thoughts on paper before we share them aloud," I said to the twelve who sat before me.

"In addition, I have a graduation surprise. I want three of you at a time to go down the hall to receive your gift. Would you be the first?" I asked as I gestured toward the three reticent managers.

"What is it?" asked Steve, the burliest of the group.

"It's a surprise!" the group gently chided him. Ten minutes later, all the time needed for this form of keep-all-your-clothes-on massage, Steve returned.

"Well? How was it?" asked one of the other managers.

"I don't think you're going to like it," he said to her as a smile stretched across his face. "So I'll just take your place."

The "ice" was broken - or should I say melted - through the warmth of healing touch.

As the group left the classroom, I announced that good-bye handshakes and hugs were both available. Steve busied himself until he was the last to leave.

After a thank-you and a good-bye hug, Steve admitted, "If only I could hug my work team, I know it would make an incredible difference."

"If you don't think people can tell the difference between a warm hug like that and a hot hug that's sexual, you're underestimating your staff," I challenged him. "You're a great hugger. Just do it."

How-to-Hug

Just as the incident with my mother-in-law revealed, many people are fearful of hugging "wrong." There is no real how-to for hugging, so you do not need to buy a book. Likewise, there is no particular "when" to hug. Anytime you need a hug you can ask for one from a friend. There are some "who's" because not everyone has learned the joy of this heart-to-heart experience. Hugging doesn't work when only one party is comfortably joining in.

There are many groups who hug so much, they offer a crash course in this form of touch. Our church is known for its hugs. At our main Sunday service each week, we have standing-room only, and our hugs are one of the reasons. I often warn those I invite about our "Hug of Peace" in the middle of the service that lasts for five to ten minutes. It's wonderful to see faces light up as arms reach out.

Listen to how often we use the phrases, "It was a touching moment," or "It just doesn't grab me." We are tactile creatures. Connecting with each other physically is one of the healthiest and most pleasurable of all our attitude adjusters.

Meanwhile, touch is not only fun for us, it's also good for those we touch. A friend of mine who speaks around the country on wellness tells her audiences, "If you don't hug your kids at home, you can be sure they'll get hugged in the back seat of a car." I find even the teens who seem too cool for this kind of warmth still appreciate a tender touch.

Safe And Healthy Ways To Stay In Touch

So where do we begin? Here are some self-starters:

1) Start small with co-workers or friends. Perhaps with a pat on the arm, or clasping both hands during a handshake.
2) Join a sports team or dance group.
3) Join a church, synagogue, temple, or support group that hugs a lot.
4) Hang around Italians or Spanish-speaking families.
5) Offer your family members, from infants to adults, a daily backrub. To make it a game, use one of the wooden massage "creatures" available at any bath or body store.
6) Begin each meeting at work with staff turning to their right and giving a backrub, then turning to their left and giving a "thank-you" backrub. Make it optional, but make it fun!

We live in a cerebral society. Many of us live our lives through our heads. We think out every situation but we do not feel them (with our heart) or sense them (with our bodies). The good news is that once we learn to live in our skin, we won't be so "absent-minded." Our minds will not be so absent from our physical bodies. We can use all our faculties to be more fully alive.

"Reach Out and Touch Someone" became a world-famous

advertising slogan in the '80s, perhaps because it appealed to our hunger for physical connectedness. In a world of law suits and sexuality fears, E-mail and fax modems, cubicles and privacy fences, it is more important than ever to stay in touch.

See me, feel me, touch me, heal me.
From the '70s Rock Opera Tommy

Habit I: Insulate From The Negatives

Comment overheard at a restaurant:
Would you like a little cheese with your whining?

Anyone who has ever watched their weight knows that simply consuming more fruits and vegetables while downing daily malts, burgers, and fries will not result in a healthy and trim body. So it is with our minds.

In order to be successful in our search for greater happiness, we must not only strengthen the positives in our lives, as we have discussed earlier. We must also become aware of helpless, blaming talk; friends whose morality choices are not in accord with ours; hopeless and helpless song lyrics; and violent and belittling images on the television screen.

Good, Better, Best

However, avoiding the negative is a task made all the more challenging by the fact that focusing on the negative or getting into judgmental thinking patterns can also increase negativity.

To return to the junk food analogy, there is nothing inherently wrong with hamburgers, french fries, or malts. Even though they are not the best for us, they are not inherently bad. Stephen Covey, in a 1994 lecture series stated, "The worst enemy of the best is not the bad. It is the good." He was pointing out that a Good vs. Bad decision is easy to make. It is when we must choose between good and better that the difficulty arises.

We can feed junk food to our brains just as we can feed it to our bodies. However, there will be a price to pay. In the past, we were unaware of the effects of words, images, and actions, just as previous generations were unaware of the negative effects of asbestos. But we can no longer claim naiveté. We all have a responsibility to heighten our awareness of those elements effecting us negatively.

Awareness Of The Big Picture

We sometimes become so inundated by the fog of negatives surrounding us that we don't realize the air is clearer elsewhere. Tina Turner's abusive husband, Ike, once remarked, "I didn't hit her any harder than my Daddy hit my Momma."

Similarly, I have heard employees make such remarks as, "Of course we have to work seven days a week. Everyone does if they want to get ahead."

Many people limit their vision of what is possible to the individuals in their immediate circle of friends or co-workers. In this case, it becomes even more important to have friends that challenge us to be more healthy, rather than less. An individual in recovery brought up the following scenario in class:

"I knew this girl was sleeping with another guy while she was dating my good friend. I wasn't sure whether I should get involved or not."

This sparked a comment from another participant:

"My best friend slept with another woman the night before his wedding day. I couldn't believe it. I felt kinda creepy standing up for him the next day." (The marriage lasted less than a year.)

As we discussed these circumstances, one woman asked, "So who are we to judge? We've all done lots of things wrong." Another added, "You can't get involved. There's too much to lose."

My questions to them were three-fold:

1) What is friendship?
2) What do you want from this friendship?
3) What price are you willing to pay?

For me, friendship includes honesty and involvement. I can't limit my involvement to the easy and good times and still be your friend. One 16-year-old girl's brother discovered that her high-school steady was also seeing a girl from another high school. The brother covered for the boy and didn't tell his sister. Who was he a friend to?

We are greatly influenced by the company we keep. When we turn off our conscience concerning a friend, we also shut down our inner direction. I do not have to judge the person when I assess the action as bad or good. To remain silent when someone does something we consider immoral is to devalue our friendship and ourselves.

I believe we become what we see, what we say, and whom we associate with. The few times I have gone with friends to a casino, for example, I have noticed very little smiling, even as coins poured out of the machines. I am leery of amusements that do not amuse.

The ratio of smoking is usually greater than 50% of the patrons, but I feel more in danger from second-hand despair than second-hand smoke. There is nothing wrong with casinos in and of themselves, but I do not believe they are in my best interest.

Tell me thy company, and I'll tell thee what thou art.
from Cervantes' *Don Quixote*

Once we become **Aware** of our choices, we can move to **Acceptance** of our responsibility to search out the best option. We then must choose **Accurate Assessments** in order to face the fears that initiating change inevitably brings. Finally, we can take an **Action** to move toward the best life offers.

Boundaries For A Better Life

In an average week, I usually find myself challenging one or two situations which most people would tolerate as "not so bad." I do this because of my goal of positive programming for my brain-computer. My assertiveness does not usually involve anger.

The first potential area of negativity I insulate myself from is destructive criticism. When someone attacks my character, as happens to all of us from time to time, I simply seek that person out and ask him or her to rephrase their criticism using the four steps in Habit A. Almost every time, the discussion that ensues brings us both to a gentler place of greater understanding.

If that person chooses not to dialogue, I simply disengage myself from their negative remarks and refocus my attention somewhere else. It is interesting that destructive criticism often comes from individuals who do not sign their attacking letters, or who will not discuss their insults further. Their fear provides the mortar for the walls of separation they have built.

There are many times in a normal week when a negative message of fear or hopelessness is telegraphed to our unsuspecting brains. We can stay alert to catch these messages and choose not to buy into them. Here are some of the steps I have taken recently to protect my attitude, my energy, and my health and well-being:

Billboards and Advertising: If I read a negative message, I protect myself from the fall-out by stating an affirmation. A billboard for Miller Lite had the slogan "Catch a Cold" right next to a beer can.
A billboard for an emergency care center read, "Tis the Season to be Sneezin'." When I see these, I remind myself how healthy I am and how grateful I am for my healthy body.

Self-talk: Author Louise Hay claims that our sub-conscious hears every negative statement as though it were about us. If I overhear an individual who is using negative self-talk, I may simply move to another area, or say something like, "Excuse me, did you hear what you just said?"

When a newly-hired secretary wrote herself a note which read, "Push the hold button, stupid!" and taped it to the phone, I asked her to remove it and encouraged her to take my class. Instead, she resigned, which seemed the best for everyone.

Movies: Not too long ago, members of my women's group and I walked out midway through a movie. We weren't thrilled with a lot of the early scenes, but when the mother of a character dismissed her daughter's resistance to dating a married man with, "You're too picky," we left. Others I spoke to said that they, too, were uncomfortable with much of the film, but wanted to stay and "get their money's worth." I believe some money is too expensive.

Music: My kids and I were visiting a friend at her cabin one afternoon, when rap music began blaring next door. We assessed that the teens' music was loud but harmless. However, when a CD full of songs using profanity came on, I suggested that the kids and I go run an errand. Instead, my friend went over and asked the neighbors to change the CD, which they quickly did with an apology. I am equally aware of the helpless messages in today's love songs. "I can't live without you," songs, for example, encourage co-dependent thinking.

Magazines: I remember seeing one publication in a physician's waiting room whose title I did not recognize. The cover read, "The Truth About the Economy." The articles inside this monthly publication described everything from dark and terrible "plots" by the IRS to global bank frauds. I asked the doctor why she had such a magazine in her office area. She said she was unaware of it.

When we take a closer look at what we see and listen more carefully to what we hear, we realize what messages we have been sending our brains. Awareness then motivates us to make changes.

I admit, we have been following the 'If it bleeds, it leads' (lead story) philosophy at my TV station.

Miami TV station director, 1995

Once Upon A Television

Easily my greatest concern regarding negativity for ourselves and our families is television. Because we have been slow to admit the effects of TV on our thinking and behaviors, its effects are all the greater.

Today families spend a higher percentage of waking time in front of the TV than in any other activity. Before the average child of today graduates from high school, he or she will have spent 15,000 hours watching television, compared to 11,000 hours in school. How does this affect us? Insidiously.

Some incidents in my own life which are telling evidence of the seductive power of television have included these:

- A few years ago, I was invited to a family dinner where the head of the table was occupied by a television set. Our entire meal was dominated by the "special" show.
- My friend's 3-year-old said she wanted a certain doll for Christmas, "batteries not included." By the time she was four, this little girl knew the line-up of shows for every night of the week.
- Not long ago I helped with a ninth-grade retreat at a Catholic high school. One of the girls in my small group prayed for "Jimmy, who died yesterday." Her girlfriend snickered and said, "The actor didn't die, just the character." We were praying for a soap opera character.

All television is educational television.
The question is, what is it teaching?
Nicholas Johnson

Because we are in a relaxed, alpha brain-wave state when we watch TV, we are even more receptive to its messages. By the age of 18, TV viewers have seen over 12,000 graphic murders and assaults.

One reason so many people feel helpless about issues such as violence is because they watch and buy into an unrealistic representation of the problem. For example, police on TV use their guns 10 times more than in real life. Once we feel overwhelmed and helpless, we give up.

A small group of committed citizens can change the world. Indeed, it is the only thing that ever has.
Margaret Mead

A three-year National Television Violence Study done by four universities in 1996 concluded that there are three major factors that determine "harmful violence" on television:

1) When we are learning to behave more violently.
2) When we are becoming desensitized to violence.
3) When we are becoming more fearful.

According to their report, the majority of TV programs today have one or more of the above elements of "harmful violence." The study also found that 73% of all television violence goes unpunished, 58% of the victims of violence show no pain, and humor - which tends to trivialize the seriousness with which violence is regarded - occurs in 39% of all violent scenes on television.

Adults and children who watch more than two hours a day of TV are not only more prone to violence, they are less hopeful, more prejudicial, and more fearful.

The Fear Factor

In a CBS *Frontline* program hosted by Bill Moyers in 1995, the claim was made that a child who watches a lot of TV (over two hours a day) begins to believe in a meaner world. "They are more afraid because they feel so vulnerable. TV creates a great amount of fear," according to their researchers. This fact is true not only for children.

Several years ago, Eva, a college student, came to America from Poland and was staying at my apartment for a few months. One evening, after I left on a date, she sat down to watch TV. When I came in, a little after one o'clock in the morning, she was sitting stiff and still in a chair in the corner. The television was on, but there was no picture, merely the white noise of a TV station signed off for the day.

I turned on some lights and saw that she had been crying. A terrifying show had traumatized her to the point that when she heard something on the roof (they have no squirrels in Poland), she was paralyzed with fear.

Television is an invention that permits you to be entertained in your living room by people you wouldn't have in your home.
David Frost

A prime example of the power of television to promote fear in children was brought to my attention after the '95 Oklahoma City Federal Building bombing. A week after the incident, a good friend of mine received a call from the Red Cross inviting her to volunteer for a special two-day counseling hotline set up in South Dakota. When I asked her why she was going to South Dakota to counsel children from Oklahoma, she corrected me. "We're counseling children from other states around the country who were traumatized by the disaster."

I reflected on the moods of my 4 and 11-year-old children that particular week. "My kids weren't traumatized," I offered for discussion.

"That's because they don't come home and turn on the television like most kids do. Thousands of children watched the replays of the disaster half a dozen times before their parents even got home."

When discussing television with parents, I often hear, "But what do you expect me to do?" The real question is, "What do you *want* to do?" We can feel like victims of our own technology, afraid to pull the plug on what we have created. Or we can remind ourselves of the spectrum of possibilities for taming the television tiger.

Reclaiming Our Power

In his book, *Six Point Plan For Raising Happy, Healthy Children,* John Rosemond states, "I don't believe there's any justification for letting a preschool child watch any television at all." Based on years of research into the deficiencies in competency skills of TV-viewing children, he recommends a limited number of quality programs only once the child learns to read.

I know many families who choose not to own a television. Still others limit the number of hours the TV is on each day. Another group of families choose to move the television out of the main family room into a room such as an unfinished basement, only bringing it upstairs for special shows.

Still other families shut off the TV around holy days, or during the summer. This hiatus gives them new objectivity toward the programs that they sometimes believe they "can't live without." The year we turned off our TV for the forty days of Lent, it took us about a week to "forget" about the tube. We didn't miss it for the rest of the season.

Setting House Rules

In addition to the consideration of how long the TV is on, there is the question of what it is showing. In our home, 90% of our viewing is public television programs or an occasional G or PG movie video. Twice in the last year we sat down at eight o'clock on a weekend evening to see if anything "good" was on the other stations. Both times, all four shows were using violence to resolve conflicts. My rule is, "If I don't want to live it, I don't want to watch it."

"No way! What would I do?" a 10 year old's answer to the *Frontline* question, "If we gave you a million dollars never to watch TV again, would you take it?"

Negativity In The Workplace

Beyond television, there are other forms of negativity to be aware of. One I'm frequently asked about is the co-worker who only has "awful" stories to tell each day at work, or who sees every situation as hopeless.

What can we do? Consider what an asthmatic would do around a smoker:

- Ask the "fuming" person to fume elsewhere,
- Move until they're done fuming, or
- Move/change jobs or departments.

There is an addiction to blame.
Each third party who sides with me about my grievance
gives me a "fix" that keeps me going.

Dr. Mary Riley,
author of *Corporate Healing*

Positives On Deck

One innovative high school teacher put a simple sign on his new deck: the word "negative" with a circle around it and a red line through it. This "No Negative" warning was so highly respected that a young married couple once rang his doorbell at ten o'clock at night to ask to spend time on the protected deck.

The faster we want our lives to change for the better, the more diligent we will become in surrounding ourselves with the best. Five minutes of affirmations will not negate hours of fear-based discussions at work. The negative aspects promoting fear and despair must be balanced by an even greater positive focus on love, courage, and hope.

None of the activities mentioned in this section are inherently bad or evil. Therefore, in confronting them, there is no need to harbor resentment if our requests for change are not granted. To do so would create more negativity.

On the contrary, because we create more of what we focus on, it is dangerous to make eradication of a negative our primary life focus. As the former creative director of Hallmark, Gordon MacKenzie, shared at a seminar I attended:

> Only the novice motorcyclist focuses on the danger of the car backing out of the driveway. That is why he has so many accidents. The veteran will keep his eyes on the goal ahead, thereby safely maneuvering around the potential danger.

We can spend our time organizing pickets against television, newspapers, magazines, movies, rap music, destructive criticism or casinos. But to create the life we want for ourselves, it is better to simply "pick-it." Once we move in a more positive direction, our environment will begin to transform itself in more positive ways. Thus, insulating from the negative will be less and less of a challenge.

Don't fight war. Create peace.
Marianne Williamson

Habit J: Journal

Journaling allows more of the totality of what we are to come alive.
G.F. Simons

Journaling. Power writing. Keeping a diary. Whatever it's called, a few minutes each day to let your inner voice speak on paper can literally transform your life. It is as simple as getting out a pen and paper. There are no rules of what to write, how long to write, or what to do with the writing when you are finished.

Why journal? It relaxes us. It "halves griefs and doubles the joys" of life when we get what is inside us outside us. Most importantly, it reveals the hidden agendas that keep us from greater fulfillment and joy.

The wisdom we connect with when we go within has been called many names: The wise old woman/man within, Sophia, the Holy Spirit, Universal Consciousness, The One. In her book, *The Artist's Way*, author Julia Cameron suggests that G.O.D. can refer to Good Orderly Direction. It doesn't matter what we call this Source. We just have to trust it is there, at all times, with creativity and happiness as its calling card.

Creativity is Divinity in motion.
Deepak Chopra

So why don't we all rush to get out our pens and pads each day? Because we know our inner wisdom exacts a high price for joy: gut-level honesty. We must face our hidden agendas. One gentleman had the courage to admit he needed more courage. "I am becoming aware that I'm not ready to become aware," he shared with the group. While admiring his honesty, we reminded him there is no way to get to the castle without first going through the dark forest.

Silence is as full of potential wisdom
as the unhewn marble of great sculpture.
Aldous Huxley

The Key To Our Basement

When we do not take the time to process the intense emotions of our experiences, we have to "store" some of the left-overs in our "basement." This is the subconscious, which most psychologists believe runs our lives. We truly "know not what we do."

That is why mental health experts agree that less than 10% of changing a behavior is will power. Over 75% of our transformation is getting to the core subconscious issue. Samuel Taylor Coleridge once wrote that no one does anything from a single motive. Journaling gets to the problem behind the problem in our basement and brings it to light. Once we know the real issue, the solution is much clearer.

The Buster Breakthrough

The power of journaling was made clear to me on a grey fall day a few years ago. I was driving home from the store when I saw our 5-month-old kitten, Buster, lying in the street. He had been hit by a car and killed. When I broke the news to my then 6-year-old daughter, we cried and hugged for quite awhile, finally deciding to bury Buster in the back yard.

Three weeks later, I came across one of Buster's toys under the couch. I sat down and wept uncontrollably. As I wept, I realized that my daughter had, by all appearances, completed her grief process. The day after Buster's death, we had bought the bird she requested, which was now the beloved family pet. Why was I still so broken up over this kitten that had lived with us only a few months? I decided to journal.

I got out a sheet of paper and began to write, "The good thing about crying so hard about Caramel's death is..." I wrote no further, as I had my answer.

Caramel had been *my* kitten who was run over when *I* was six. The day of the accident, my well-meaning parents had told me not to cry for fear of upsetting the younger children or increasing the sadness of my uncle who had been behind the wheel of the car. Had I not journaled, I might not have become aware of the need for healing this powerful childhood memory.

Journaling can write your childhood wrongs.
Catherine L. Taylor,
author of *The Inner Child Workbook*

Often, as we begin to journal, our subconscious takes over, revealing insights that can help us make decisions, calm our fears, or make more sense of our past. Once we turn off our TV channels, the channel that goes 24 hours a day within us has many secrets to reveal.

How To Begin

As with any habit, it is helpful to prepare mentally and physically for journaling. You may want to make a commitment with a friend that each of you will take five minutes a day to write for one week. Or you may want to go out and buy a blank book to keep your writings in. Preparation of any kind increases your likelihood of following through with your goal.

To begin, I always date my entries, even if I am writing on a napkin that I plan to throw away as soon as I leave the restaurant. This step calls me to "be here now" and gets me started writing. The first words always seem the most challenging to get onto paper.

Beyond that, I don't suggest any one technique for journaling. One woman shared that the previous night she journaled just one word, "Damn!"

A gentleman shared that one evening he wrote down, "I do not want to journal tonight," then continued to write for four very illuminating pages!

When I journal, I can:

- write in poetry or pig-Latin,
- doodle for days or dangle my participles,
- write a letter to myself, to God, to my boss, or to a deceased relative.

Journaling is simple, but once again, not always easy.

Get out of the way....
Accumulate pages, not judgements....
Leap, and the net will appear.
Julia Cameron

Barriers to Journaling

As simple as the process of journaling is, most of us still balk at the thought of it and rush to our excuses:

1) **"I'm afraid I'll do it wrong!"**
Despite my objections, one woman in my class was adamant that she had "done it wrong." Upon further inquiry, she admitted she had written with a pencil and erased! Her classmates encouraged her to find a safe hiding place for her writings and change from pencil to pen.

   When you are finished, if you still have qualms about your papers ending up in the wrong hands, you might use a burning ritual as you express your gratitude for the wisdom and freedom of the journaling experience.

2) **"I can't find the time."**
No one has ever "found" 5-10 minutes a day. Time must be set aside. Stephen Covey points out that if we do not make time for what is **important**, but **not urgent**

(journaling, rest, relationships, exercise, etc.) we will find our lives consumed by what is **important** and **urgent** (illness, arguments, accidents, crises).

3) **"It would be like Pandora's box. Too much would come out!"**
This reference to the Greek myth of the woman who opened a forbidden box only to turn loose the demons of the world reminds me of a recent divorcee in one of my classes. "I think I'd kill him if I journaled!" she argued. I suggested that her chances of killing him were greater if she did not journal.
I recall a speaker who came to my high school class to talk about drugs. He said that the subconscious is like our basement. We store the overflow joys, anxieties, and sorrows there. He said the psyche "brings up" things from our basement slowly, never giving us more than we can handle... unless we are on a drug like LSD. "Then the drug rips a hole in the psyche and we get inordinate amounts of joy or pain." If we are not on LSD, we are safe.

------------------------ EXERCISE ------------------------

If you have already experienced journaling, you know the rewards it can bring. For the novice, here are 15 Journaling Ideas to get you started.

1) **Write the highs and lows of the day.**
2) **"I am becoming aware..." (Complete it 5 times).**
3) **Make a gratitude list.**
4) **"In a perfect world..." (Complete the phrase, filling one side of a sheet of paper).**
5) **Write 3-6 endings each for the following phrases:**
   "I am..."
   "I realize..."
   "I want..."
   "I will..."
   "I know..."

6) Complete the phrase, "I feel most comfortable when..."
Complete the phrase, "I feel most uncomfortable when..."

7) Complete the phrase, "If I were willing to see what I see and know what I know..."

8) Get out a picture of yourself. Describe what you see in detail.

9) Write down four qualities you admire in others. Now attribute them to yourself. For example: "I am caring, conscientious, honest, and a good friend."

10) Ask your body to speak to you. What is your back telling you? Your head? What are your feet telling you? Your eyes? Your hands?

11) Remember back to the last compliment you received. Write it down word-for-word five times in first person.

12) Write the eulogy you would like read at your funeral.

13) Write the word "Journaling" five times down the left hand side of your paper. Then write a sentence about journaling after each. For example: "Journaling is..." or "Journaling feels...."

14) Write on truth. How important is truth to you? When are you most truthful? What feelings or actions are the most difficult for you to accept? To write about? To admit to others?

15) Visualize tomorrow going really well. Now pretend it is the day after tomorrow. Write down your description of your wonderful yesterday in detail, looking back on what a great experience it was!

When you are finished, you may hide or destroy your journaling, but congratulate yourself on writing!

Journaling is house-cleaning. It differs from thinking about something, which just rearranges the heirlooms and junk in our attics. Writing out our thoughts and feelings is the equivalent of giving a whole bunch of stuff to the Salvation Army. It gets our feelings out of our gut and onto paper.

There are many ways to house-clean our inner selves: A therapy session, a walk with a close friend, a nervous breakdown. However, journaling is the easiest and most accessible tool for doing it on a regular basis.

If you bring forth what is within you,
what you bring forth will save you.
If you do not bring forth what is within you,
what you do not bring forth will destroy you.

Gnostic Gospels

Habit K: Keep On Keeping On

The only thing that stands between you and grand success in living are these two things: Getting started and never quitting!
Dr. Robert Schuller

We are an instant society. We like fast food, fast cars, and fast cures. We have surgery rather than change our life style. We get a divorce rather than see a counselor. We do faxes, E-mails, and World Wide Webs for instant access.

I admit it, I'm smitten too. This book came out one year later than I originally planned because I broke it into smaller chapters. I realized that I prefer my books in bite-size chunks so I can digest them more quickly. I assumed many of you would feel the same way.

Perhaps the most alarming component of our instant-society is that we are betting more and more money every year in hopes of becoming "Instant Winners." The truth is there is no such thing. All winning takes time. All winners are patient.

Most people give up just when they're about to achieve success. They quit on the one yard-line. They give up at the last minute of the game one foot from a winning touchdown.
Ross Perot

Learning takes time. Loving takes time. Living to the full takes time. How have we forgotten these important life truths? More importantly, how can we remember them? The dedication of this book referred to every teacher as a gardener. Perhaps the simplest way to remind ourselves and our children of the value of patience is to start a garden. When my son grew his first plant in a plastic cup, he would check it every day for progress. The only thing that kept him from spooning that dirt into his piles in the back yard was our daily reassurance that a sprout would emerge. When the grass grew, it was sacred to him, his very own "miracle." His next planting project was not nearly so challenging.

Faith in a seed, in ourselves, in a program, or in a higher power is one of the most important ingredients for a healthy and happy life. Once we have faith, we will have patience. Once we have patience, we will have success.

Nothing in the world can take the place of persistence. Talent will not....Genius will not....Education alone will not. Persistence and determination alone are omnipotent.

Calvin Coolidge

The other lesson a garden teaches us, besides faith, is faithfulness. A garden begun and then left untended can overwhelm a plot of land, resulting not only in low yield, but a high workload at the end of the summer. Once we see the first fruits of our labors, we cannot stop working the garden, or the program, that brought them forth.

I am often asked if I am faithful to exercise, meditation, journaling, and affirmations every day. I have done each of these daily for a year or two at different times in my life. Now, I can say that I do at least one of the above every day. I vary them with my needs, desires, and schedule. The other skills I use every day - hugging, praying, optimistic thinking, asking for what I want, monitoring self-talk, limiting media, showing gratitude, singing, smiling, and reading motivational literature - have surely changed my life for the better.

Each individual's personal program will be worked in his or her own unique way. But it must be worked *for years* to yield long-lasting results. Too discouraging? We have all been brushing our teeth daily for years, when the only real feedback is a good report from our annual trip to the dentist. Your level of success depends on your level of commitment.

So how do we learn patience and persistence? By facing the three greatest enemies to Keeping On Keeping On: boredom, discomfort, and surviving the rocks.

This thing we call "failure" is not falling down, but staying down.
Mary Pickford

#1: Boredom

I had the opportunity to interview a four-time NCAA champion wrestler not long ago. When I asked him to tell me about the hard times, he spoke of the boredom. "My dad and my coach were always on me to practice the fundamentals, when I wanted to practice the more exciting stuff....Their coaching won me the championships. On the days when I was really tense or so tired I couldn't see straight, my body still remembered the fundamentals from all those drills."

Finding our motivation from the excitement of the long-term goal, rather than from the excitement of the moment, results in the pay-off of persistence. We can use our imagination to feel the feelings of our eventual success as easily as we can recall the feelings of our last disappointment. By using our imagination to play over and over the possible "success scenarios," boredom won't have a chance.

#2: Discomfort

Carolyn Myss, in her audio tape, *Why People Don't Heal*, displays a disdain for those of us who whine whenever we feel uncomfortable.

> You must take the program in your mind and drop it to your will and shove it down there and say, 'This is what you will do. You will get up in the morning and exercise everyday for an hour. I don't care how you feel, you will do it.'

> You begin to take these things your mind knows and force yourself to live them, no matter how uncomfortable you are. When you get stuck, say to yourself, 'Comfort is not my business; healing is.' It is irrelevant that you are tired, uncomfortable and exhausted. Who cares?

This challenge flies in the face of modern day conveniences. A friend of mine is on his annual fishing trip as I write this. He and his group will get up very early tomorrow morning, climb into a boat, and hope for hungry fish. "The call of the wild" will excite their all-male crew with the smells of adventure in their Canadian surroundings. Then, just a few hours into their outing, other smells will excite them. The host will drive up in a small boat, bringing fresh fruit, rolls and coffee. Roughing it nowadays seems to mean no room service.

#3: Surviving The Rocks

Recently, I suggested to my fifth grader that she do her hero report for school on Wilma Rudolph. From her research, my daughter learned that Wilma had to fight tremendous odds to achieve success. She was born premature, the twentieth of 22 children. She was raised in severe poverty and had to deal with the racism of the '40's and '50's. She also came down with polio, making it impossible for her to walk without braces until the age of eleven.

Wilma credits her mother's wisdom as the key to her ability to overcome obstacles and sustain a positive attitude. "My mother taught me very early to believe I could achieve any accomplishment I wanted to." Fueled by great persistence, as well as a dream of a better life, Wilma became the first woman to earn three gold medals in track at the 1960 Olympics.

Wilma Rudolph's over-comer story is similar to so many: Charles Barkley in basketball, Colonel Sanders in the restaurant business, and Abraham Lincoln in politics, to name just a few. The message for us, and for our children, is that every challenge in life can make us better or bitter. The greater the felt-pain, the greater the potential success.

When you get into a tight place and everything goes against you, and it seems as though you could not hang on a minute longer; never give up then, for that is just the place and time that the tide will turn.

Harriet Beecher Stowe

The Dream That Would Not Die

Of all the overcomer stories I have read, perhaps the one most vivid for me is the story of Gary Willie. Gary was a young black teen who had no money for college in the '60s. His only hope was the recruiter who came to his high school each spring to choose one or two young men for an athletic scholarship.

The day of the try-outs, Gary gave his all but was not selected for the honor. His best friend was chosen instead. The day he waved good-bye as his friend left for college on the bus, Gary ran to his coach's office, sobbing. "I've got to go, Coach. All I've ever dreamed of was going to college."

"How much money do you have, Willie?" asked the coach.

"About twenty dollars."

"That's enough for a one-way bus fare. Take your money and go to your college."

Gary did just that. He hid out in his friend's dorm room, eating food his friend snuck out of the cafeteria. Every day he would show up at practice and go through the drills on the sideline. Every day he would ask the coach for another chance, and every day he was told to go back home.

Near the end of the summer, Gary decided to try one more thing. He had his friend sneak him into the locker room, where he hid in an empty locker. When everyone had gone home that night, he climbed out and scrubbed the room until it shone.

When the coach walked in the next morning, he smiled, heaved a sigh, and told Gary to come into his office. There he said he would personally pay the student's $10 registration fee and offered him a scholarship, but only for one year.

One year became four, and Gary Willie got his degree. So,

how did I hear about him? I read a one-page article in People magazine. Gary Willie, attorney-at-law, had just donated $10 **million** dollars to Shaw University, the largest individual donation to an alma mater to date.

Progress, not perfection.
The AA Big Book

Commitment to a friendship, a cause, a community, or a course of action can only come with the knowledge that every step makes a difference in the final outcome.

Not long ago, a 48-year-old counselor was having lunch with her hair stylist, when the former revealed why she was no longer counseling. "I'm pregnant...with twins!" It was her first pregnancy, but her third marriage. "Every painful lesson I have learned until now has been worth it," she shared with her friend. "Now that I know how happy I can be, I wouldn't change a single thing leading up to this moment."

------------------------ EXERCISE ------------------------

Ask yourself:

- **Would I have written off a counselor who had two "failed" marriages?**
- **When and why do I tend to write people off?**
- **When and why do I tend to write myself off?**
- **How many positive events need to happen before I trust someone or something?**
- **How many negative events need to happen before I stop trusting?**

Wait-power

Working the program described in this book does not require

much will power. It is more about patience and persistence, what I call "wait-power," as we change the way we think about ourselves, others, and life.

Fall seven times, stand up eight.
Japanese proverb

Have you noticed how many quotes there are in this section? I could list quotes of thousands of men and women recognized for their great achievements, because most of them have, at one time or another, spoken of or written on the importance of persistence. Of all the threads that connect writings on changing your life and improving your attitude, perseverance reigns as the strongest determinant.

Inch By Inch

Whether it be for a gold medal or for a golden opportunity, each dream is achieved one step at a time. As I type these words, I pray that you, too, will add a paragraph to your dream text, and that you will always remember that it is darkest just before the dawn. Meanwhile, keep with you the words of those who have achieved so much before us: *Never Give Up*. Or, as an earthworm might put it: "By the inch, life's a cinch, so Keep On Keeping On!"

Have patience with all things, but chiefly, have patience with yourself.
St. Francis De Sales

Habit L: Lighten up and Laugh

You grow up the day you have the first real laugh - at yourself.
Ethel Barrymore

We don't need a magnifying glass to see the humor-happiness connection. Come on, face it. You opened this section hoping for a couple of good jokes. Okay, okay...but before I give you my favorites, I want you to figure out yours.

------------------------ **EXERCISE** ------------------------

Think back to three or four of the funniest incidents in your life or the lives of those you know. Write down some key words on a sheet of paper, like:

1) Wedding dress caught on fire from candelabra.
2) Driving through car wash with sun roof open.
3) Laughing so hard I fell out of the boat.

Now, think back to the three or four funniest jokes or stories you've ever heard. Write those down as key phrases also.

Humor And Our IQ

Professor Howard Gardner's research concluded in the 1980s that there were actually seven areas of IQ: math, verbal, kinesthetic, musical, spatial, intrapersonal, and interpersonal. His work has sparked amazing insights into the variety of combinations of gifts in the human community. Recent studies now indicate that there is an eighth area as well: *a sense of humor IQ*.

Because my main gift is intrapersonal, this book is about understanding ourselves. But we all have at least a small gift in each of the areas. Just as we want to exercise the math and verbal areas of the brain to keep them in shape, it is important to keep our sense of humor toned up as well.

Seen on a refrigerator magnet:
A waist is a terrible thing to mind.

Since sense of humor is not one of my naturally strong areas, I have to work at it. That is, if you can call listening to Stephen Wright and watching the video *Airplane* annually "work!" I also use cartoons, comedy shows, refrigerator magnets, and humorous articles as humor stimulants from time to time.

With the completion of the first exercise in this section, you now have a "funny file." I keep mine handy for whenever the mood hits. Just as I often have cravings for Mexican food, sometimes I just have to rent a Jerry Seinfeld video. Just as I may go to a movie to help me cry, I may also go to a comedy club to help me laugh.

Laughing and crying are actually extremely closely connected. Look back to your list of funniest real-life occurrences from the above exercise. In every instance, the person involved could have laughed or cried. The difference between the two is simply one of distance.

In the early '90s, singer-songwriter Bette Midler crooned, "From a distance, the world looks blue and green...." The song goes on to say how much calmer and more peaceful things would seem if we would look at them from afar. Laughter is "getting some distance" on an incident we might be tempted to take too personally.

The true personal life incidents I'll be sharing with you on the upcoming pages were all potentially mortifying experiences. Thank heavens laughter helped us all survive them.

Incision Derision

A friend of mine I'll call Billy, (so he'll stay a friend of mine) had an embarrassing moment during his senior year in high school. The teacher at his parochial school was covering various religious rites with her seniors.

On this particular Friday, she asked a hypothetical question, "You all know what circumcision is, don't you?" Immediately, Billy's hand flew up in the air. Since Billy didn't speak up all that often, the teacher was curious about what he wanted to add to the discussion. "Yes, Billy?" she asked.

"It's when they cut the skin off your forehead," Billy offered. According to my sources, I am told that was the last comment he made in class his senior year.

What's All The Hoop-la?

At a party for our pastor's anniversary, we had a hula-hoop contest for all ages. It was simple: if you kept the hoop going longer than anyone else in your group, you made it to the finals.

Being an athlete and a bit of a perfectionist, a dear friend of mine went into her round with gusto and determination; so much so that when they played the music for her to begin, she "hula-ed" the hoop right over her head. You could say she really hooped it up! (Very punny!) I laughed so hard I could barely breath.

Caught At The Christmas Crib

The week before Christmas things are always bustling around our house. The year my daughter Joanna was eleven we put out the Nativity crib in our sunroom, a room she played in often. One evening that week I was in the dining room wrapping packages when I heard her exclaim from the sunroom, "Jesus!"

Hardly able to believe I had heard such profanity from my eldest, I spoke to her, but her back was to me and she didn't hear me. "Jesus!" she said again. Horrified, I went in and asked Joanna what the problem was. She held up the baby figurine in the manger and said, "We're going for a ride and he won't get in his car seat!"

Oh Brother

On the Monday after his Mom delivered a little girl, 5-year-old Timmy returned to kindergarten. "I've got a new baby sister!" he proudly exclaimed to the teacher as he walked into the classroom that morning.

"I heard about that, Timmy," said his teacher. "You must be very excited."

"Yup! But it's the last one," he noted.

"Oh, really?"

"Yup! Mom had her boobs tied."

If it's sanity you're after, there's no recipe like laughter.
Henry Rutherford Elliot

Love and Laughter

Laughter can be serious business. When Rita was preparing for marriage, she and her fiancé took a course for couples where one of the instructor's comments was, "Laughter in each other's presence is one of the best signs of a healthy relationship." She pulled the presenter aside at the break and admitted that she and her intended did not laugh when they were together. "Oh, just nerves before the big day," she was told. Five years later, when I met her in the shelter, she told me she had never been able to laugh in her husband's presence.

Wit is the only wall between us and the dark.
Mark Van Doren

I once saw a plaque that read, "Know why angels fly? They take themselves lightly." So how do we lighten up? Hang around with funny people. Listen to a comedian's tape. Follow our "wild hairs" when we get a silly idea.

One of my favorite fortieth birthday parties was one where each of us was given an assignment from Judith and Richard Wilde's book, *101 Ways to Stay Young*. We had people walking with pop cans on their feet; playing kazoo combs; wearing half dollars as monocles; making fish faces; and wearing napkin bras. And we were all sober!

One of the reasons people consume so much alcohol in America is so we can let our hair down. The goal as we become healthier and happier is to become so self-comfortable that we can do the fun things we used to explain under the guise of "I was drunk."

Recently, in a class I was teaching for recovering addicts, a young man named Pat reminded me that in order to stay sober, we can't be too "sober."

I had walked in that morning in what I term my "Caribbean dress," and received many "oohs" and "ahs." As I was thanking a woman for her compliment, this strapping Irishman asked, "If I ever decide to cross-dress, can I borrow it?"

Humor is the hole that lets a little sawdust out of a stuffed shirt.

Anonymous

Humor is one of my tests of a good friendship. I have a tendency to be unorganized, and it has been amazing to watch the different reactions to my admitted weakness.

Back when my corporation was non-profit, our newly hired executive director railed at the board one meeting that I was "terrible unorganized!" After a slight pause, one board member pointed out, "If she wasn't, we wouldn't need you, now would we?" She was not in the position for long.

On the otherhand, my choir loves my idiosyncracies, and wastes no time teasing me about them. After a concert not long ago, one member interrupted a gentleman's praise of my work with, "Yes, she's gifted, but don't put her on a pedestal! Next week we're sending her to a class for the Organizationally Impaired!"

When I start to get down about my weaknesses, I love to remind myself that Einstein was called "a moron" by many of his peers while growing up. My favorite story took place while he was a passenger on a train.

As the story goes, the conductor walked up to take his ticket and watched as Einstein frantically searched through his pockets for the important item.

"Oh, Dr. Einstein," the conductor blurted out. "I didn't realize it was you!" He went on to say what an honor it was to have such a guest aboard his train, as the prestigious passenger continued his desperate search.

"Sir, I don't need your ticket. Sorry to have bothered you," the conductor offered.

"*I* need my ticket!" Einstein exclaimed. "I don't know where I'm going!"

I know that for every door that closes,
another one opens, but these hallways are the pits!
Refrigerator magnet

Sex Is Not A Four-Letter Word

On a day-to-day basis, the most important key to humor is to just relax. Through humor, we can safely discuss what is difficult to talk about. That is probably why sex is the focus of so many more jokes than any other topic.

It's so important to feel our feelings.
When I want to cry, I think about my sex life.
When I want to laugh, I think about my sex life.
Glenda Jackson

Sex is also a popular topic for humorous books, as are cats, computers, and cosmetic surgery. Just a stroll down the humor section of your local bookstore is worth a few giggles as you read titles like the following:

- *Politically Correct Bedtime Stories*
- *Still Pumped From Using the Mouse*
- *David Letterman's Book of Top Ten Lists and Zesty Lo-Cal Chicken Recipes*
- *Don't Squat With Your Spurs On*
- *You're Only Old Once*

I also got a kick out of such parodies as:

- *Sports Imitated*
- *The Book of Vices*
- *Women Who Love Cats Too Much.*

So, go read a funny book, or take a funny friend out for pineapple right-side-up cake. Then, consider these suggestions:

- Listen to a comedy tape on your way to work.
- Post cartoons around your home and office.
- Read the funnies.
- Have a puppet in your car for traffic jams. Then put on a show for all the other drivers stopped in traffic.
- Wear colorful suspenders.
- Go to a park and play on the swings and slides.
- Give a silly name to a machine you work with or drive.
- Tickle someone.
- Wear sexy underwear. (Or...???)
- Smile. (It changes the chemistry of every cell in your body.)
- Buy a desk toy that winds up or pops.
- Leave a mystery message on your co-worker's / supervisor's answering machine.
- Have a "take your child to work" day. Okay, maybe only half a day!
- Sing in the shower or at a karaoke bar...but don't quit your day job!
- Organize a "Guess-The-Baby-Pictures" contest for your co-workers.
- Have a stress ball handy for when someone needs to

squeeze the air out of something! (Drawing someone's face on it is optional!)
- Go skinny dipping or play ice ball, depending on the climate.
- Put a goofier than Goofy message on your answering machine.
- Every time you hear a good joke, write it down and leave it on three other people's answering machines.
- Buy M&M's and throw them at unsuspecting passersby.
- Stand waiting to greet the garbage collection team with drums, horns, party hats, and a sign that says, "Just a *litter* message to say THANK YOU!"

Life is too important to be taken seriously.
Anonymous

A good friend of mine is a veterinarian who writes wonderfully humorous poetry for his talks to his peers. He shared with me recently that he had a really hard time in college, and the thing that got him through was being chosen the class "Critic" two out of his four years. This was the student whose job it was to make fun of the programs and professors. He went on to explain, "It absolutely saved me. I couldn't have done it without the perspective that humor offered."

If we think about it, to let go of worry and "not sweat the small stuff" is to live the carefree life of a child. No one laughs as often or as long at absolutely nothing than a child. When we laugh, we live and love better. Laughter is good for the soul, the body, and the "never mind."

S/He who laughs, lasts.
Bumper Snicker

V. SHIFT HAPPENS: TOOLS FOR TRANSITION

Definition of Insanity:
Doing what you've always done
and expecting different results.

There you have it: My top 12 Habits of Happiness. Choose one thing you've learned here and begin it <u>now</u>. Here are some final tips on what to expect during the transitions.

How Change Happens

Some behavioral researchers say it takes 21 days of repeating a new behavior daily to create a habit. Others say 14 days. Still others say it takes 12 months to see real progress. Whatever the amount of time needed to make a lasting change, it is neither instant nor eternal. When we are faithful to the goal of health and happiness, "shift" happens. An important step in making positive changes is in altering how we think about change itself.

I remember the day I ran to my counselor because I was back-sliding. I had been free from my pattern of binge-eating for about six months, when a week of chaos and crisis hit. I lost my bearings, ate a huge package of potato chips, and sat totally discouraged in his office as I told him of the experience.

"Mary Kay," he shared, "habits are like canyons. You had an old canyon of binge eating behavior; now you've been digging a new canyon of healthy eating habits. You need to realize two things:

"First, your new canyon isn't as deep as your old one. That means when you get all turned around by a problem, you will still naturally return to the old canyon. Secondly, the dirt from digging the new canyon isn't filling up the old one. The old one will stay with you forever. Your goal is to get the new canyon deeper so that you automatically resort to a healthier set of behaviors."

"How long do I have to wait for the new canyon to be deeper?" I asked.

"You've been binge-eating for about seven years, so I'd guess around seven months or so."

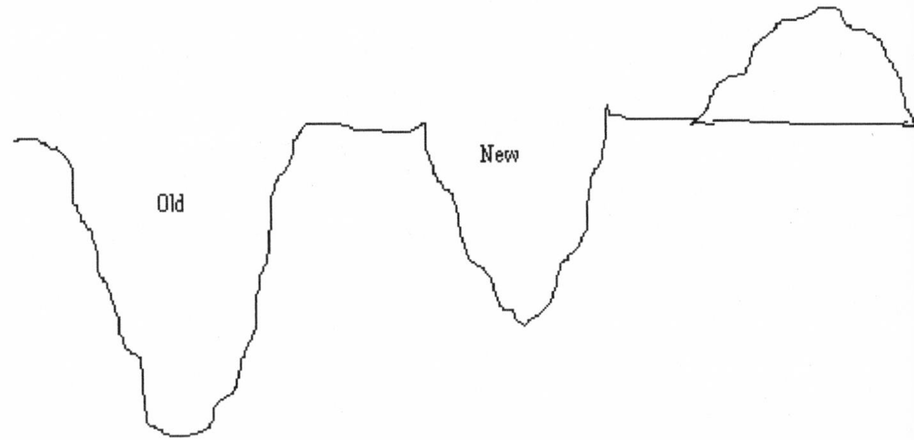

I truly appreciated his formula: One month of the new for every year of the old. It helped me to be patient with the process. Often I see people who read a book and believe they are then "fixed." We just aren't programmed that way. I have seen miraculous, seemingly overnight turn-arounds, but I know that the new behaviors didn't come overnight. There were many dark nights of the soul that were encountered along the way before the new lifestyle could stick.

On the lighter side, look at how a toddler becomes potty-trained. First, he doesn't even notice the "mess" has happened. He keeps wondering why the living room or the bedroom smells so bad! We, too, sometimes wonder why life "stinks," overlooking the true source of the problem.

Next, the toddler figures out: The smell is coming from Me! Once he discovers what behavior is creating the problem, he tries to change overnight. But, oops! Sometimes, it's in the middle of doing things the old way that the moment of awareness occurs. Finally, the little one successfully catches himself before the "accident" occurs, and changes his behavior!

No one faults a toddler for taking time to make the transition. We can decide to be just as patient with ourselves.

Measuring The Magnitude Of Change

There are three ways to go about change. For some, like me, the all-at-once dramatic change works best. For others, starting small is more helpful. So let's look at the advantages of each size of change.

For our purposes, I'll use the analogy of shedding our skin to describe the size of changes we can make.

1) The lobster way is dramatic and complete.
2) The snake way is more gradual, in layers.
3) The human way is constant and in very small increments.

The Lobster

The lobster, like many of us, resists change. It builds a wall around itself in the form of a hard shell, and only changes when its "inner growth" causes too much pain to tolerate. Once the lobster outgrows its shell, however, huge, dramatic change is no longer merely a choice. It is the only means of survival. The lobster will suffocate if it does not change. Thus, the creature cracks its shell and crawls out, leaving all of its safety behind until it grows a new shell.

I have seen men and women who have gone through similar dramatic changes in their lives. Their pain is so intense that they release what seems to be all of their old beliefs and behaviors in one fell swoop.

I'll always remember the attractive woman in her 30s who yelled out "Yes!" at the end of her first two-hour class with me. Four classes later, she shared with us that she quit drinking and kicked out her abusive boyfriend that first evening. (I saw her a year and a half later and both changes were still in place!)

While this dramatic, instantaneous change is exhiliarating, there is much danger due to vulnerability. As with the lobster, it takes a long time for this new "self" to become solid. We learn quickly to care less about what others think, because this kind of change attracts attention and we have to get used to dealing with it.

The good news is that, just as the lobster's new shell is larger, these individuals also move into a new, more expansive consciousness that benefits them for life.

The larger changes, because they set clear boundaries and have fairly immediate, dramatic results, are more difficult at first. But they are usually easier to maintain.

Change is not made without inconvenience,
even from worse to better.
Samuel Johnson

In changing my diet to more low-fat choices, I learned a lot from a book/tape by Dr. Dean Ornish called, *Eat More, Weigh Less*. He states that "Comprehensive changes are easier to sustain than moderate ones." It's easier to stop eating red meat altogether than to cut down, for example, because of the immediate rewards of having done so. Often we feel better, more energized immediately. As Ornish states, "Joy is a much more powerful motivator than fear."

The Snake

The snake chooses a less exciting approach to change, shedding his skin in layers. He waits until a summer's day when the heat becomes uncomfortable and then slides out of one coat of skin at a time.

When we have put off making changes in our lives, this shedding becomes necessary. For one individual, it might be asking for a much deserved raise; for another, asking a room-mate to smoke outside. These changes are not usually earth shattering, but they can definitely increase our heart rate as we go through a time of transition.

I recently overheard parents of a teen-ager complaining about having trouble with their son. Upon inquiry, I discovered they were still using the "because I said so," response to his questions. This technique is fine for four and five year olds who can't understand all the "whys" of rules and discipline, but it's inappropriate for older children. Once we practiced some new ways of listening and sharing, the parents were willing to shed old behaviors for a new, fresher approach. Although uncomfortable at first, these moderate transitions can yield very encouraging results.

The Human

Finally, there is the way you and I shed every cell of our skin every year. This process is so natural to us that we are not even conscious that it is happening. Yet none of our skin cells are more than twelve months old!

Lived out, this pattern would be embodied by people who are comfortable with change, who "go with the flow" more easily than their peers. They non-aggressively speak their opinions on a regular basis. When change doesn't find them, they look for change.

A good example of this is someone who reads publications to keep up on the latest news in their interest area, or someone who continues to challenge themselves physically by jet-skiing one year, running a half-marathon the next, and sky-diving the next. People who are comfortable with change tend to enjoy travel because it continues to stretch them and help them grow.

With this attitude toward change, there are fewer big risks needed because of the smaller ones taken along the way. If we put off change, we face having to "shed" everything at once. Then we feel naked, as I did when leaving my marriage and beliefs about myself years ago. If, on the other hand, we allow the sometimes painful truths of life to transform us on a daily basis, staying open to new ways of thinking and acting, our soaring to new heights will be a lot smoother.

Once we change our minds, the behavior changes will come. There will be some pain and anxiety along the way, but they are no match for the reward that awaits heroes like ourselves at the end of the journey.

What is death to a caterpillar,
to the butterfly is being set free.
Anonymous

In Conclusion

All of life's problems originate within, either from

1) Fear,
2) Despair, or
3) Judgement of self and others.

With that understanding, the keys to happiness are clear:

1) Courage,
2) Faith and Hope, and
3) Loving Acceptance and Forgiveness.

I grew up hearing about love and happiness from family and church, frustrated that I had no formula for either. Now I know that the formula is composed of the simple behaviors we have discussed here.

These lessons are not new. They have been passed down through the ages for each generation, each individual to rediscover and express. We can not do otherwise. Even on our darkest days we are learning the lessons of love and happiness. We are right where we're supposed to be, today, this moment. Life and learning are the great adventures. Love and happiness are the great rewards.

Robert Louis Stevenson once said, "There is no duty we so much underrate as the duty of being happy." I hope that this book has reminded all of us of our responsibility to pursue happiness; not in the clinging to things or people, but in the following of the gentle, winding path of our hearts' desires.

We do not need to create happiness. It is within us each moment, longing for expression. Happiness is our destiny. All we need do is come home to it.

Good Journey.

About the Author

Mary Kay Mueller, the proud Mom of Joanna and Zachary, is a popular international speaker and consultant on empowerment, team building and communication skills. Honored as a Heartland Hero in her hometown of Omaha, Nebraska, she is a professional member of the National Speakers Association.

Also known for her singing voice and compositions, Mary Kay has produced three cassettes of her songs as well as a 3-part video series, "Letting Your Light Shine," available through her company, INsight INc. This book is her latest step in living out INsight INc.'s Mission Statement:

To call forth the wisdom and courage of persons of all ages to value themselves and others.

To get on her mailing list for future books and tapes, send in the form or call us at the number below.

Please Let Us Know Of Your Stories!

This book is filled with the success stories of the thousands of individuals who have benefitted from Mary Kay's program. We'd like to hear yours, too.

Send questions, comments, anecdotes, poetry, etc. to:

INsight INc.
P.O. Box 6470
Omaha, NE 68106-0470

Or Call us at 1-800-419-0444

Or E-mail us at insightmkm@aol.com

READING LIST

Branden, Nathaniel. *Art of Self Discovery (The).* New York: Bantam Press, 1993. Easy to understand explanation of the powerful sentence completion technique, ie. "The good thing about. . ."

Hartman, Cherry. *Be Good to Yourself Therapy.* New York: Thomas Nelson, Inc., 1994. Tiny little book with a ton of wisdom.

Canfield, Jack and Mark V. Hansen. *Chicken Soup for the Soul.* Deerfield Beach, Florida: Health Communication, 1993. 101 true inspirational stories from the world's top motivational speakers.

Beattie, Melody. *Co-Dependent No More.* St. Louis: Harper Hazelden, 1987. Includes a checklist of co-dependent characteristics.

Gawain, Shakti. *Creative Visualization.* Mill Valley, California: Whatever Publishing, 1986. Helpful in learning to create a vision.

Lerner, Harriet Goldhor. *Dance of Anger (The).* New York: Harper & Row, 1985. Shows how *we* are responsible for playing a part in our own anger or the lack of anger on the part of others.

Jeffers, Susan. *Feel the Fear and Do It Anyway.* New York: Fawcett Columbine, 1987. Awesome book for getting past fear.

Burns, David. *Feeling Good.* New York: Penguin, 1981. Excellent book for learning about inaccurate assessments or for dealing with depression.

Powell, John. *Fully Human; Fully Alive.* Niles, Illinois: Argus Communications, 1976. All his books are wonderful. This one focuses on overcoming inaccurate assessments.

Hendrix, Harvel. *Getting the Love You Want.* H. Hold, 1988. Marriage manual that teaches us to get to the core issues in our relationships and to ask for what we want.

Powell, John. *Happiness Is An Inside Job*. Allen, Texas: Tabor Publishing, 1989. Wonderful supplement to this book.

Cousins, Norman. *Head First: The Biology of Hope.* New York: E.P. Dutton, 1989. Focuses on hope, humor, and self-responsibility. Many amazing stories of recoveries and remissions.

Bradshaw, John. *Healing the Shame that Binds You.* Deerfield Beach, Florida: Health Communications, 1988. On the difference between guilt about an action and shame about our inner core.

Branden, Nathaniel. *Honor the Self.* New York: Bantam Press, 1990. One of his many wonderful books.

Colgrove, Melba, et al. *How to Survive the Loss of A Love.* Lea Press, Inc., 1991. Small book with 58 pages of specific tips, poems, and exercises to do while grieving the loss of love.

Sher, Barbara. *I Could Do Anthing if Only I Knew What It Was.* New York: Ballantine Books, 1989. If you're not sure what your dream is.

Rasberry, Salli and Padi Selwyn. *Living Your Life Out Loud.* New York: Pocket Books, 1995. Fun guide to greater creativity.

Forward, Susan. *Men Who Hate Women and the Women Who Love Them*. New York: Bantam, 1987. Answers your questions about whether your marriage/relationship is verbally abusive or just difficult.

Fankhauser, Jerry. *Power of Affirmations (The)*. Farmingdale, NY: Coleman Graphics, 1983. Guide to affirmations.

Branden, Nathaniel. *Psychology of High Self Esteem (The).* Tape series. Call 1-800-525-9000 to order. Includes many journaling exercises offered in Mary Kay's program.

Peck, M. Scott. *Road Less Traveled (The).* New York: Simon and Schuster, 1978. Excellent primer into the biggest questions of why and how.

Clifton, Donald O. and Paula Nelson. *Soar With Your Strengths.* New York: Dell Publishing, 1992. "Find out what you do well, and do more of it. Find out what you don't do well, and stop doing it."

Helmstetter, Shad. *What to Say When You Talk to Yourself.* Shows you the power of positive self-talk and instructs you on how to create your own self affirmation tapes.

Louden, Jennifer. *Woman's Comfort Book (The): a self nurturing guide for restoring balance in your life.* San Francisco: HarperCollins, 1992. Short chapters, excellent suggestions.

Norwood, Robin. *Women Who Love Too Much.* Los Angeles: Jeremy P. Tarcher, 1985. For getting out of abusive situations.

Hay, Louise. *You Can Heal Your Life.* Carlsbad: Hay House, 1984. Covers the body-mind connection and why we feel the way we do.

For Families with Children:

Rosemond, John. *6 Point Plan for Raising Happy, Healthy Children.* Kansas City: Andrews & McCeel, 1989. Practical, common sense guide to parenting for this generation.

Now that you've heard Mary Kay's message of hope, you'll want to share it with friends!

To order by phone, call 1-800-419-0444

The 4 A's of Affirmative Living: From Attitude to Action This 4 cassette tape/workbook set will help you to discover how to unlock your hidden gifts, change bad habits for good, and improve communication skills to enhance your relationships, job, & health. **$45.00**

Getting a Head Start A 60-minute cassette that we fondly dub "a swift kick in the attitude." The beginning of helping you learn to value yourself and change your life. **$12.00**

How to Raise (the Self Esteem of) Our Children This 50-page booklet of practical wisdom, compiled by Mary Kay Mueller, is an invaluable guide for parents and teachers **$6.00**

INsight INk Newsletter This bi-monthly newsletter helps you keep up with the latest from Mary Kay Mueller. Price covers a 1-year subscription. **$10.00**

_____ **Considering having Mary Kay as a speaker for your next event? Check here and we'll send you a PR packet and/or video!**

Name ____________________
Address ____________________
City ____________ **State**____________ **Zip** __________
Daytime phone____________________
(area code + phone number)

QTY	ITEM	COST	TOTAL
		TOTAL DUE:	

Method of Payment (check one)

____Check ____MasterCard ____VISA

Account Number ____________________
Name on Account ____________________
Expiration date ____________ Amount Charged ____________
Signature ____________________

Please mail to: INsight INc. P.O. Box 6470 Omaha, NE 68106-0470

Or call 1-800-419-0444